A Teacher's Life:

Stories of Literacy, Teacher Thinking, and Professional Development

James A. Muchmore

A Teacher's Life

Stories of literacy, Teacher Thinking, and Professional Development

By James A. Muchmore

Copyright 2004 by James A. Muchmore

Published jointly by
Backalong Books
    Box 33066, RPO Quinpool Centre
    Halifax, Nova Scotia, B3L4T6, Canada
Caddo Gap Press
    3145 Geary Boulevard, Suite 275
    San Francisco, California 94118, U.S.A.

Cover photograph, Grailville, Ohio
    by James A. Muchmore
Cover template by Punch Productions
    Alan Barbour and Ted McInnes
    Halifax, Nova Scotia, Canada

ISBN 1-880192-47-0 (US)
ISBN 1-984132-12-2 (Canada)
List Price $25.95 US; $28.95 Canada

4320

Library of Congress Cataloging-in-Publication Data

Muchmore, James A.
    A teacher's life : stories of literacy, teacher thinking, and
professional development / James A. Muchmore
        p. cm
Includes bibliographical references and index.
    ISBN 1-880192-47-0 (alk. paper)
1. Education--biographical methods--Case studies. 2. Language arts
teachers--United States--Psychology--Case studies. 3. Language
arts--United States--Case studies. 4. Education--Research--United
States--Methodology. I. Title

    LB1029.B55M83 2003
    370'.7'2--dc21
               2003012130

CONTENTS

ACKNOWLEDGEMENTS

Writing this book would not have been possible without the support and encouragement of many colleagues, friends, and relatives. First and foremost, I would like to thank J. Gary Knowles, Pamela Moss, Arnetha Ball, and William Alexander for their assistance in bringing this project to completion. I am especially thankful for the patience and guidance afforded by Gary Knowles and Pamela Moss; their support over the years has been invaluable.

I would also like to acknowledge the "Self-Study of Teacher Education Practices" and the "Lives of Teachers" Special Interest Groups of the American Educational Research Association for the inspiration they provided. My friends and colleagues at Western Michigan University deserve acknowledgement too.

Finally, my family has provided me with a great deal of encouragement. I thank my mother, Rosemary Muchmore; my father, Ronald Muchmore (who died shortly before this book was published); and my sister, Angela Patz, for all of their loving support. Lastly, and most importantly, I would like to thank my wife and friend, Elaine Sayre. This book would never have come to fruition without her.

PROLOGUE

Autobiographical writing helps us to explore and understand the thoughts, motives, and biases that guide our actions. It provides the means for us to reflect on who we are, understand where we have been, and imagine where we might go. It enables us to examine in depth our public and private selves as we continuously create and recreate meaning in our lives. For researchers, this kind of self-scrutiny can be extremely useful in developing research agenda, formulating theories, conducting studies, and reporting findings. Yet, academic discourse has traditionally excluded "the personal." Indeed, including one's personal story in academic writing has long been deemed inappropriate, with the resulting text being dismissed as unprofessional, unreliable, and solipsistic.

Recently, however, some educational researchers (and others) have begun to recognize the value of using autobiography as a way to understand human experience and to gain a deeper understanding of oneself (see, e.g., Ayers, 1992a; Ceroni et al., 1996; Cole & Knowles, 2000, 2001; Diamond, 1991, 1992, 1993; Lee, 1994; Li, 2002; Loughran & Russell, 1997; Mahabir, 1993; McCallister, 1998; Neilsen, 1998; Soler, Craft, & Burgess, 2001; Trapedo-Dworsky & Cole, 1996). For example, Diamond (1991) maintains that we all make up stories about ourselves in order to live. "By constructing our narratives," he states, "we make sense of our world and our place in it."

> Through self-narratives we can devise and consider other alternative, possible realities. If we are to control and direct our own thinking and teaching lives, both which are fictive processes, we must begin by becoming more conscious of them (p. 90).

Similarly, Randall (1995) suggests that a life can be viewed as an unfolding novel—one in which we are simultaneously the author, the protagonist, and the reader. We make it up as we go, he says,

> ...living forward yet understanding backward; ceaselessly adjusting our sense of what sort of story it is, of where it is going, and where it has been; weaving now this "accident" or "mistake" and now that into what we think is the plot; playing now with this anticipated future or remembered past and now with that; trying to see now this causal connection between events and now that—wondering not only "what next?", that is, but also "why?" (pp. 205-206).

If our lives are evolving stories, then autobiography is more than just a tool for facilitating self-understanding; it is, in fact, an integral part of everything that we do—including our research. All researchers bring their personal stories to their work. The topics they select, the questions they ask, and the methods they choose are all heavily influenced by their personal life histories. Consequently, it is not only appropriate to include autobiographical and personal writing in academic discourse, but it is important to do so—for to leave out "the personal" is to leave out an integral part of the research itself.

This book is about Anna Henson,[1] an experienced high school English teacher with whom I collaborated in a multi-year study of teacher thinking. Using ethnographic, life history, and narrative approaches, I explored the history and evolution of Anna's beliefs about literacy, teaching, and students, and how these beliefs influenced the pedagogical decisions that she made throughout her career. However, it is more than just a study of Anna. It is also a study of myself.

In traditional forms of research writing, the researcher tends to exist as a shadowy figure, absent from the text, known only by his or her name beneath the title and perhaps through a brief biographical sketch at the end. While some researchers deviate from this tradition by writing in the first person, I have moved a step further by framing my entire study as an autobiography. Who am I? Why did I choose to do the study? How has it influenced my life as a researcher and a teacher? These are some of the questions that I address in my work.

Background of My Study with Anna

I first met Anna in 1990 when we were both enrolled in a graduate course that focused on authentic literacy assessment. Anna was a fellow doctoral student at the University of Michigan as well as a full-time public school teacher in Detroit. The course was structured more like a working research group than a formal class; each week we explored issues concerning student writing, accountability, and portfolio assessment. Throughout our weekly meetings, we regularly shared our insights about writing, students, and teaching in general—and we grew to value the reflective wisdom that Anna brought to the table. With almost 25 years of experience as a classroom teacher, she exuded a quiet confidence in her teaching. Whenever she talked about her classroom, I never sensed any of the underlying dissatisfactions and frustrations that I had experienced as a teacher, and, as the semester progressed, I found myself increasingly wondering how she had gotten to this point in her career.

The course culminated in a classwide presentation of our work at the Annual Meeting of the American Educational Research Association (AERA). Afterward, instead of disbanding, several of us accepted an invitation from Anna to collaborate with her and a few of her colleagues at Windrow High School[2] in Detroit. We decided to focus on student writing, authentic literacy assessment, and teachers' professional development. My research with Anna arose in the context of this initial collaboration.

Approximately five months after our work at Windrow began, I was required to conduct a semester-long ethnographic study for a course that I was taking on qualitative research methods, and I needed both a site and a topic. Since I already had access to Windrow, I decided to dovetail this course assignment with my ongoing work there. All I needed then was a research question. Having just completed a large-scale survey study of teachers' beliefs and practices (Muchmore, 1994), which involved more than 1000 Chapter 1 teachers[3] in my home state of Kentucky, I was interested in pursuing a similar topic for the research course—only this time I planned to use a qualitative approach and focus my attention on just one teacher. Given my ongoing relationship with Anna, as well as my previous curiosity about her career as a teacher, she seemed a logical choice. What were her beliefs about reading and writing? What did she do in her classroom? To what extent were her beliefs and practices related? How had this relationship been mediated by the teaching contexts that she had experienced throughout her career? What kinds of pedagogical decisions had she made in response to such contexts? These are some of the questions that I formulated while initially conceptualizing the study.

When I presented my rough idea for this study to Anna, her first reaction was one of surprise. As a private person, genuinely modest about her teaching practices, Anna would probably have preferred not to draw attention to herself through this kind of a study. However, because she trusted me as a colleague, and perhaps because she felt some sense of obligation to me as a friend and a fellow graduate student, she ultimately agreed to participate. At the time, however, neither of us could possibly have imagined the ultimate scope and complexity of such an undertaking, which ended up spanning more than five years and eventually evolving into this book.

Throughout my study, I conducted numerous audio-recorded interviews and conversations with Anna and made frequent visits to her classroom in the role of a participant observer. Under Anna's direction, I also spoke with several of her friends, relatives, colleagues, and past and present students—all of whom were familiar, to varying degrees, with her teaching practices and her outward thinking about literacy. In addition, Anna provided me with a collection of academic papers that she had written throughout her career in which she had discussed a variety of issues related to literacy and teaching. She also provided me with copies of an assortment of professional documents—including newspaper clippings about her, and past and present evaluations of her teaching conducted by her supervisors. Taken together, all of this information enabled me to construct an in-depth portrait of Anna's life as a teacher with a particular focus on her beliefs and practices.

Organization of the Book

I began to write this book with the intention of focusing solely on Anna. Initially, I had no intention of framing my work as an autobiography. The more I wrote, however, the more I realized that my study of Anna was actually as much about myself as it was about her—for it was through my own life experiences that I was ultimately making sense of hers. In addition, I gradually realized that one of the most powerful implications of this kind of study was the way in which my thinking about teaching and learning was influenced by our collaboration. Throughout successive drafts, more and more of myself kept creeping into the story, until I finally decided to frame the entire document as an autobiography—with my study of Anna being nested within the larger context of my own life history. The resulting text is divided into three parts, plus an epilogue and an appendix.

Part I, which consists of Chapters 1 and 2, is a personal narrative dealing with my life as a student, a teacher, and a researcher. These chapters introduce several themes that are important for understanding my work with Anna. For example, there is the story of my grandmother, which provides an insight into the connection that I drew between her and Anna. I was very close to my grandmother, who died in 1985, and Anna was somewhat like her, both in her personality and her bookish interests. This comparison helps to illuminate the kind of relationship that Anna and I developed—as the researcher and the researched, the younger and the older, and the mentee and the mentor. I admired Anna, just as I admired my grandmother, and I viewed her as an important mentor in my attempt to better understand my own experiences as a teacher.

In addition, there is the story of my transition from a quantitative researcher to a qualitative one. Before beginning my work with Anna, my thinking was deeply rooted in the scientific paradigm, and it took me a while to fully appreciate the nature and value of interpretive inquiry. In addition, because the impetus for my study with Anna lay in a large-scale survey study that I did in Kentucky, and because the theoretical basis for my work with Anna emerged from a body of literature on teacher thinking that was largely quantitative, I feel that it is useful to draw a distinction between these very different approaches to research.

Part II, which consists of Chapters 3 and 4, includes a review of the literature on teacher thinking that served as the impetus for my initial collaboration with Anna. This literature is characterized by an eclectic array of methodologies, divergent foci, and idiosyncratic terminologies—all of which make it very difficult to synthesize (e.g., Clark & Peterson, 1986; Elbaz, 1991; Fenstermacher, 1994; Kagan, 1992). In order to contextualize my research, I provide an overview of the main strands of the literature, with a particular focus on those studies that most influenced my work with Anna. These studies include the work of researchers such as Barr and Duffy (1978), Buike and Duffy (1979), DeFord (1985), Duffy (1981), and Hoffman and Kugle (1982), all of whom utilized survey methods in studying teachers' conceptions of reading and writing. At the end of Chapter 3, I briefly describe my own survey study that I conducted in Kentucky (Muchmore, 1994), highlighting the shortcomings of using surveys to study teachers' thinking.

In Chapter 4, I discuss the epistemological underpinnings of the life history approach that I used in my study with Anna. Here, I maintain that our lives are textual, in that we make sense of them through narrative and that the process through which we create meaning in these narratives is very similar to, if not nearly the same as, the process through which we create meaning in written texts. To illustrate my growth as a researcher, I relate two particularly poignant experiences or epiphanies (Denzin, 1989a)—one in an art museum and the other in a troubling interaction with a former mentor. I conclude this chapter by addressing some of the common criticisms of life history research regarding validity, reliability, and generalizability.

In Part III, which includes Chapters 6 and 7, I present Anna's life history. It is by no means a comprehensive account, for my goal was not to delve deeply into her personal life or to explore every facet of her career. Rather, it was simply to provide readers with a general sense of who she was, where she came from, and how her life evolved—especially her life as a teacher. I pay particular attention to the history and development of her teaching practices and her underlying beliefs about literacy, teaching, and students. In addition, drawing upon my fieldnotes, newspaper articles, photographs, and other archival data, I weave various contextual information throughout my narrative, thus situating Anna's beliefs and practices within a broader historical context. This attention to context is a key characteristic of life history research.

In the Epilogue, I explore the implications of my study. Although an in-depth life history study of the beliefs and practices of a single teacher has little value for making generalizations about other teachers in a statistical sense, it can be extremely useful as a vehicle for elaborating our understanding of our own beliefs and practices. Donmoyer (1990), for example, makes a compelling argument for expanding our conception of generalizability to include the learning that we experience when we read about single cases. By reflecting on my life as a student, a teacher, and a researcher—in addition to telling Anna's story—my study not only helps to build theory, but it also provides readers with a useful tool for reflecting on their own professional lives and practices.

Finally, in the Appendix, I discuss the methods and ethics of my work with Anna. It is divided into three sections. In the first, I present a detailed inventory of all the information that I gathered in my study with Anna. In the second section, I describe the strategies that I employed in analyzing this information, while in the third section I discuss some of the ethical considerations that Anna and I encountered throughout our work together.

A Teacher's Life

PART I

PERSONAL STORIES

In the two chapters that make up this part of the book, I establish the context of my work with Anna through an extended account of my own story as a teacher and a researcher. This piece of autobiographical writing had its origins in 1992 when I was teaching a reading and writing methods course for preservice teachers at the University of Michigan. One of my assignments was for students to form writing groups and compose literacy autobiographies. I participated too, writing a brief, three-page account of my own personal literacy history. Several weeks later, when everyone had finished, we compiled our writings into a class anthology, which then became an important classwide text for us to read, study, and learn from. Several years later, I returned to this piece of writing and continued to work on it, until it ultimately spanned more than 50 pages and formed the first two chapters of this book.

In Chapter 1, I present an account of my early life, tracing my interest in life history research to the family stories that my grandmother told, and showing how this narrative way of knowing was later usurped by my interest in science. Next, I relate a story from my first year of teaching, detailing some of my frustrations and pointing out the discontinuity that I felt between what I had been taught as a preservice teacher and what I was experiencing in my classroom. Finally, I discuss my life as a student, including my transition from a chronic underachiever in elementary and middle school, to an honor student in high school, to my decision to become a teacher in college.

In Chapter 2, I reflect on my life as a preservice and beginning teacher. Drawing upon old notes, papers, course syllabi, and coursepacks, I describe what I learned in college, with a particular emphasis on my beliefs about literacy. Then, returning to the story of my first year of teaching, I re-interpret this experience in light of my more recent thinking about literacy. Finally, I conclude this chapter by relating some of my frustrations as an inservice teacher and explaining some of the events that led me to return to graduate school.

It is important to note that these two chapters do not represent a definitive autobiography per se. I believe that such an undertaking is impossible, for my story is constantly changing and evolving as I continually interpret and re-interpret the remembered events of my life—sometimes emphasizing one experience, other times another, always basing my choices upon the perceived importance of a particular experience at a particular point in time. In other words, the story that I narrate today is not the same story that I would have told yesterday, nor will it be the same story that I will tell tomorrow. There will be similarities, to be sure, but events and experiences that I now deem significant may become less important to me in the future, just as I may one day choose to emphasize aspects of my life that I do not discuss here. I may even forget a few things, or I may end up reinterpreting a past event in light of some new experience, thereby assigning it an entirely new meaning.

Five, ten, or twenty years from now, I imagine that I may be embarrassed when I go back and reread these chapters—embarrassed by the story that I have chosen to tell, compared to the story that I may then be inclined to tell. It is much like viewing an old photograph of myself as a teenager. "Yes, it's me, but I don't look the same today." Writing freezes our thoughts and our lives in much the same way that photographs freeze our physical images. Therefore, I caution readers to be aware that although my story may appear to be nicely ordered, comprehensive, and complete, it is actually only one version—one that is fraught with all the limitations of time, text, memory, and my own purposeful selectivity.

CHAPTER 1

EARLY LIFE

My story begins with my grandparents. Their home was always a special place for my sister and me. Although they lived in the same town in Kentucky, only about a mile away, going to their house was like traveling to a different world—a world full of books and stories and timeless serenity. Unlike our parents' house where my sister and I typically fought and argued, our grandparents' home exuded a tremendous aura of tranquility, punctuated only by the rhythmic ticking of the antique cuckoo clock that hung in the family room. It was a soothing place—safe and comforting—and whenever my sister and I visited there, all of our sibling conflicts magically vanished.

My grandmother was a serious reader, and the entire house was set up to accommodate this activity. The walls were lined with shelves that were stocked with all kinds of books—old and new, large and small, paperback and hardcover. There were books on almost every topic, ranging from philosophy, to theology, to history, to fiction, with many of them reflecting my grandmother's strong devotion to introspective thought. There were works by authors such as Goethe (1808-1832/1941), Steiner (e.g., 1926, 1933, 1959), Jung (e.g., 1939, 1957, 1958), Merton (1948, 1949), and Filmore (e.g., 1947, 1953, 1960)—all with well-worn pages and my grandmother's steady underlinings of various words or phrases.

There were also many children's books. My sister and I both had our favorites—hers usually being long and challenging, like *Heidi* (Spyri, 1945) and *Little Women* (Alcott, 1869/1947) which she read as an eight-year-old, while mine were generally much shorter and simpler, like *Little Toot* (Grumatky, 1967), *The Little Engine that Could* (Piper, 1930/1961), and *The Three Billy Goats Gruff* (Asbjornsen & Moe, 1957). I was a year younger and less precocious.

Now, more than thirty-five years have passed, and both of my grandparents have long since passed away. Yet, I can still see my grandmother sitting in her chair next to the window, quietly absorbed in a book, my grandfather softly snoring in another chair with an open newspaper sprawled on his lap, and my sister sitting on the divan, thoroughly engrossed in her book. Meanwhile, I am lying on the floor hastily flipping through mine, looking at the pictures more than the words, and enjoying the peaceful atmosphere as much as the book itself.

Sometimes, my grandmother offered us other kinds of stories—those of our family history. Sitting on the divan with my sister and me at her side, she would captivate us with stories about our ancestors. It did not matter that we had heard them all many times before. Each version was slightly different and offered us new insights into the lives of people whom we eventually came to know as if we had met them in person. For example, there was her great-great-great grandfather, a Revolutionary War veteran from Maryland who lived to be 102. Crossing the Appalachian Mountains at the age of 70, he came "out west" to Kentucky with two sons and bought a farm. The large cedar trunk that carried their belongings had been handed down from generation to generation, and it now rested in the corner of the family room just a few feet from where we sat.

There was also her paternal grandfather, an Irishman from County Cavin, who fled the Potato Famine as a teenager and eventually settled in Northern Kentucky, where he became a Methodist minister. He too lived to a ripe old age, and he played a very important role in her early life. It was he who provided her with spiritual guidance and inspired her lifelong love for books.

Her other grandfather, however, was quite a different story. An embittered old Confederate, he was mean and crotchety—still angry about the South's defeat in the Civil War, even though the conflict had ended 50 years earlier. My grandmother had but one memory of him—sitting on the front porch with a cane at his side and angrily swiping at her or any other children who happened to venture too close. Although he generally avoided traveling north of the Ohio River, he had made this one exception to visit his daughter in Cincinnati, and my young grandmother and her friends had unknowingly offended him by singing a patriotic song they had learned in school. It included a refrain about General Sherman's "march to the sea."[4] The old man was outraged. Turning to his daughter, he angrily exclaimed, "This is what happens when you raise your children in a damned Yankee country!"

In addition to these stories, my grandmother also kept what she called her "trinket box." It was a tattered old jewelry box that contained an eclectic assortment of family items she had accumulated over the years. Inside, there was everything from hat pins, to baby shoes, to an old pair of wire spectacles. There was also money, some of it dating to the 1830s, as well as ration stamps from the Second World War, various pieces of costume jewelry, and a collection of empty perfume bottles that still contained traces of their former fragrances. Finally, there were old photographs—both paper and tin-type—which depicted many of the characters who appeared in my grandmother's stories. One picture, for example, showed her beloved Irish grandfather as a young man, seated in a chair with his wife standing at his side. They looked like a happy couple, she with a faint smile on her face and he with a bright twinkle in his eyes. Then, in another picture, he was suddenly much older and by himself. His shoulders were stooped and his face was wrinkled and covered by a long white beard. His eyes, nevertheless, still displayed that same youthful spark. My sister and I loved going through this box, trying to piece together the stories that it contained.

At the time, however, I did not consider what we did to be research. Research was something that scientists did. It was supposed to be cold, hard, impersonal, and objective—and researchers were supposed to be intellectually engaged but emotionally detached. Researchers were not supposed to be passionate about their "data" lest they compromise their objectivity. In retrospect, I feel that this conception of research was formed through the high value that society places on science and was reinforced through my years of schooling. Throughout my formal education, there was always an implicit assumption that knowledge gained through empirical-analytic research was vastly superior to that which was gained through personal experience. The former was trustworthy and indisputable, while the latter was unreliable and idiosyncratic. In such a world, there was no place for the stories that my grandmother told.

Rocketships, Science, and Schooling

Given the era in which I grew up, it is not surprising that I developed a reverent attitude toward scientific research. Born on the day before John

Glenn's historical flight around the earth in 1962, I grew up in the shadow of NASA's[5] Apollo space program. During my early years in elementary school, I remember being enthralled by the television images of Apollo 11 landing on the moon, and my friends and I spent countless hours pretending we were astronauts. "What do you want to be when you grow up?" someone would ask. "An astronaut!" I would shout. I was no different from most of my friends in this respect. We all wanted to be astronauts. I still remember the excitement that we felt when our second grade teacher began the school year by telling us that she had been in Florida that summer and had actually witnessed the launching of Apollo 11. We were truly in awe to be in the presence of someone who had seen, firsthand, what we had all so excitedly watched on television.

The next summer there was Apollo 13, and I again sat in front of the television set, this time quietly transfixed by the life-or-death drama that unfolded before me. There had been a terrible accident in space, and we were told that the astronauts might not get back to earth alive. Tragedy was averted, however, by some quick thinking by the NASA scientists, not to mention the astronauts themselves, and I remember breathing a long sigh of relief when it was all over and I could happily go back to watching re-runs of *Lost in Space* and *Star Trek*. Just like the fictional worlds of the Robinson family and the Starship *Enterprise*, where science always prevailed, to me the real world of Apollo 13 was a place where science reigned supreme.

Later, in high school, I learned about the scientific method. First, you consider a problem. Then, you formulate a hypothesis. Next you design and conduct a study and objectively record the data. Finally, you systematically analyze this data and draw conclusions. Six easy steps. That was all there was to it. It sounded so neat and simple—and correct. After all, wasn't that how we had developed the knowledge that enabled us to reach the moon? By using the scientific method? With science, it seemed, anything was possible.

As a preservice teacher, I encountered little to challenge my way of thinking about science and research. Instead, it was continually reinforced by virtually all of my courses, all of my reading, all of my professors, and all of my experiences. Throughout my preservice teacher education, schools were regularly depicted as highly-structured, highly-ordered, and highly-predictable places, where interchangeable teachers systematically imparted knowledge to groups of interchangeable students. Of course, the message was never conveyed in quite those words but it was there nonetheless. It was there in nearly everything that I did. Scientific-sounding words such as "experiments," "subjects," "treatments," and "controls" dominated the educational research literature that I was required to read, and I learned about a host of objectively-proven teaching techniques, ranging from models of assessment, to programs of instruction, to systems of rewards and punishments. My job, as I clearly saw it, was to master a body of knowledge that had been systematically discovered and mapped out by groups of educational researchers who had utilized the scientific method. And, because this idea of research fit so well with what was then my intuitive sense of the way things were supposed to be, it was something that I did not question.

In my first year of teaching, however, I experienced a rude awakening. Hired as a special education teacher in a small town in rural Kentucky, I quickly learned that schools were anything *but* highly-structured, highly ordered, and highly-predictable places. In my classroom, I was confronted with a group of twelve and thirteen-year-old children who could not read or write—at all—and who came from families where no one else could read or write. What was I supposed to do? How was I supposed to teach them? Nothing seemed to work—none of the models, none of the programs, and none of the elaborate systems that had been so highly touted when I was in college. Teaching, I discovered, was much more than simply implementing a set of procedures that had been deemed "correct" by the experts. It involved the lives of children—not just their lives as students, but their lives outside school as well. And it involved the lives of teachers too. Teaching, I discovered, was a very complex undertaking, fraught with a great deal of uncertainty and filled with many problems for which there were no simple solutions. And science did not hold all the answers.

The biggest problem that I experienced as a beginning special education teacher was with classroom management. I spent the majority of my time working with students who were identified as having severe behavior problems, and some of them were extremely difficult to handle. There were frequent emotional outbursts and temper tantrums as the students continually battled with me and with each other. Several years later, after I had entered graduate school at the University of Michigan, I wrote about one of my most troublesome students. The following excerpt conveys some of the frustrations that I felt at the time, and which I still think about today.

Joyce first entered my classroom as a new student on a Tuesday morning in the middle of October. The principal was grasping her arm with one hand and holding a thick manila folder in the other as he led her down the steps into my basement classroom. "Good luck with this one," he said with a heavy tone of sarcasm in his voice. "You'll need it." Then, after plopping the folder onto my desk, he hastily retreated back upstairs to the safety of his office. I was a first-year teacher, and I was a newcomer to the community. The principal's words were still fresh in the air when Joyce gave me a defiant glare and shouted, "I ain't gonna do no work!"

The community in which I worked was a vestige from the past. With a population of less than 800, it stood like a small island surrounded by vast fields of corn and tobacco in rural Kentucky. It only had two dozen streets, each bordered by large and small wooden frame houses that had mostly been built in the Nineteenth Century. In fact, it would be fair to say that not much had changed in this town during the past hundred years, and it was easy to imagine how it must have looked when those houses were new. People sat on their front porches in the evening and waved at the occasional passing cars—habitually checking their watches at the sound of the evening freight train that lumbered through the town each day at precisely the same time.

Perhaps the biggest event to have occurred in the history of this community was the building of an interstate highway in the late 1960s. Passing by the east side of town, it had turned the community into a convenient exit, and the town had prospered. In recent years, there had arisen two large gas stations, a truck stop, and even a small motel, each of which was a strong asset to the local economy. The highway came up frequently in conversations too, with the local residents often using it as a convenient way to mark the passage of time—much like their forefathers had probably used droughts, floods, blizzards, and other significant acts of nature. They frequently referred to past events as having occurred before or after the highway.

At first, I had assumed that Joyce was also a newcomer to the community, perhaps a transfer student from a neighboring school district. Dressed in a t-shirt and blue jeans, she looked like a typical twelve-year-old. While it was obvious that her family did not have a lot of money, she did not really appear to be that unusual. However, I soon learned that she had lived in the community for her entire life, frequently moving from one address to another, and that it had taken school officials six weeks to find her and force her to come to school.

Joyce had a violent temper and had established herself as the school bully. Using her mouth and her fists, she fought with the boys as well as other girls. Many of the students were afraid of her and did their best to stay out of her way.

Throughout the next few weeks, I had several long, un-fruitful meetings with the principal and the school psycholo-gist to discuss ways in which to handle Joyce. It was almost impossible to control her, and I knew she was not learning anything. Joyce was in the sixth grade—yet she could not read or write, other than naming a few sight words and print-ing her name.

In trying to deal with this situation, my first impulse was to call her parents—but they had no phone. I tried writ-ing notes and sending them home with Joyce, but I never got a response. Every Friday, I gave each of my students a weekly progress report to be signed by a parent and returned on Monday—but Joyce never brought hers back. Then, one morning, she ran into my classroom and proudly announced, "I have my progress report today!" I smiled as she handed it to me, but I immediately noticed that it was not signed. "Thank you for bringing your report back," I said, " but I see that it is not signed." She replied with a hurt look on her face, "But it *is* signed! Don't ya see mah daddy's mark?" I looked again and saw a large "X" scrawled across the bottom of the sheet. I became embarrassed as I suddenly realized that her father could not sign his name. I paused for a moment and then silently wondered, "But if he can't write, then how was he able to read the note?" Gathering myself, I looked at Joyce and posed my question aloud. She smiled and exclaimed, "Oh, I read it to him. I told him it said I was the smartest girl in the class and that I was doin' real good!"

When I announced the date of the parent-teacher con-ferences, Joyce loudly complained, "Mah daddy cain't come n'less it's dark outside! He don't have no license, and he's afraid the sheriff'll catch 'im if it's light!" In recent weeks, I had learned that Mr. Green worked at the local truck stop, and I decided to call him there. At first, he was quite upset that I had bothered him at work, and he absolutely refused to come to school for a conference or anything else. He almost hung up on me, but I finally convinced him to stop by "just for a few minutes." Joyce's story gained credibility when he said that he could only come after nightfall.

Mr. Green was a tired-looking man with a permanent scowl etched on his face. Probably in his late forties, he looked much older. His eyes were like two dark holes, set deeply in his head, and a tattered old overcoat hung loosely on his narrow shoulders. "Why don't you just whoop her?" he grumbled in a deep, gravelly voice when I expressed my concern about Joyce's behavior. His question was punctuated by an intense coughing spell, and he took several deep breaths before he continued. "I whoop her all the time, and she minds me!" I tried to explain that Joyce was a bright girl with a great deal of potential, but I left school that night simply hoping that she would not be beaten because of our meeting.

Joyce once told me that her father had been expelled from school when he was in the second grade, and that he had never gone back. "He was just too ornery for them teachers!" she exclaimed. "I'm ornery too!" Indeed, I sometimes found myself working with her on a word bank, a language experience story, or some other reading activity, when she would suddenly jump out of her seat and shout, "Ahh don't wont tuh do this!" Then she would rip the cards or paper to pieces and glare at me with intense hatred in her eyes....

Struggling from day to day trying to survive in this job, I found myself looking not to the educational research for answers, but to other teachers—and to my own past experiences as a student. All around me, the other teachers in the school had very traditional approaches to classroom management. Their classrooms were teacher-centered, and they dealt with behavior problems head-on. If a student misbehaved, then they usually overpowered him or her through sheer intimidation—either by yelling threats, or by sending him or her to the principal's office. The principal was an imposing figure, very stern and authoritarian, and students were deathly afraid of him.

Although I found this approach to be distasteful, I too began to use it. After all, it was what the students were used to, and it was what they expected. It was also very similar to the treatment that I had experienced when I was a student.

Life as a Student

For nine years—from kindergarten through the eighth grade—I attended a small, private school in Kentucky, which had a total enrollment of less than 150 students. Begun in 1955 as a rigorous, old-fashioned, "back-to-the-basics" alternative to the public schools, it emphasized intensive phonics instruction, proper penmanship, good citizenship, and corporal punishment. Many of the teachers had received their initial teacher training during the 1920s and 1930s, and some of them had already taught for thirty or more years in the public schools before joining the faculty. For the most part, they were extremely conservative in their thinking about education. Strongly resenting the social and political upheavals of the late 1960s and early 1970s, they longed instead for a return to the idealized past when standards were clear, teachers were respected, and students behaved.

The school always had a strong elitist atmosphere. It prided itself on being "better" than the public schools—an attitude which apparently still exists there today. I recently received an alumni newsletter which stated the following:

> [The school] has remained miraculously anachronistic in the areas of academic excellence, student discipline, and integrity. Throughout many years of educational and social upheaval in the public sector, [it] remained insulated and even isolated from the chaos around it. It simply continued with tried and true methods and standards in the classroom, resisting the temptation to jump onto the bandwagons that come down the road on quite a regular and predictable basis.

I remember an incident in the early 1970s when one of my teachers got distracted from the lesson at hand and began to talk about the local public school district's "ill-fated" experiments with open classrooms. Just a couple of years before, the public school district had built a new junior high school, not far from where my family lived. It was a strange-looking building when it was completed—a sprawling, single-story, windowless structure with giant exposed steel trusses and I-beams that were painted fluorescent pink and green. My sister and I had always laughed at it whenever we rode by, at first, that it was even a school. It certainly did look odd. We laughed again when we learned that it did not have walls on the inside. Who had ever heard of anything so ridiculous? A school without walls! The teacher laughed too, as she mercilessly criticized the whole concept of open schools. At the time, I did not know what she was talking about. What exactly was an open school? The teacher simply told us that it was a wrong-headed idea that did not work, and now after spending hundreds of thousands of dollars to build this new school, the public school board had finally come to its senses and decided to put in the missing walls. If they had not been so carried away by this whole fad of open schools, the teacher suggested, then they would have built the right kind of school in the first place and saved local tax payers the added expense of having to pay for these new walls. At the time, her argument seemed indisputable.

Most of the students who attended my school came from wealthy and influential families. One of my schoolmates was the son of the incumbent governor of Kentucky. Each day, the little boy was chauffeured to and from school by a uniformed state police officer who also served as his bodyguard. My parents, on the other hand, were neither wealthy nor influential. Instead, they had chosen to send my sister and me to this school mainly because they had not liked the way my sister had been treated at the local public school. Being surrounded by books as a young child, she was already a fluent reader by the time she entered public school, and the teacher was upset because the first-grade curriculum consisted almost entirely of teaching the students how to read. Not knowing what to do with a little girl who was already reading lengthy novels while the rest of the class was still mastering the alphabet, the teacher had angrily informed my parents that they had "ruined" my sister by allowing her to read so early. In response, my parents abruptly removed her from this public school and enrolled her in the private one. There, they thought, she would benefit from the smaller class sizes and the more individualized attention—which she did. My sister became an excellent student, eagerly doing whatever the teachers asked of her and always receiving straight *A*s on her report card.

My parents were so pleased with my sister's experience at this private school that when it came time for me to enter kindergarten, they decided to send me there too. Unfortunately, however, I did not have the same positive experience. I hated the school. I hated the regimentation. I hated the control. I hated not being able to talk. And I hated being yelled at, and sometimes hit, for not paying attention. At my grandparent's house, stories and books had always been fun, but at this school they were dull and boring. Day after day, it was always the same routine—read the chapter, answer the questions, do the workbook pages, and listen to the teacher—and year after year, my teachers always repeated the same refrain: "Jimmy has the capability but does not work up to his potential. Why can't he be more like his sister?" Making good grades was important to me. I wanted to be a good student like my sister, but it seems that I was labeled early on as an underachiever, and, once having developed that reputation, it followed me throughout the school. My teachers *expected* me to be an underachiever, and like Pygmalion's famous sculpture, I lived up to their expectations.

In spite of my negative feelings about this school, my parents never considered sending me anyplace else—nor did I ever express a desire to leave. Strange as it may sound, as much as I disliked this school, I also enjoyed it—at least certain aspects of it. I enjoyed the extra-curricular activities, such as doing projects for the science or history fairs, performing in our annual Gilbert and Sullivan productions, and running foot races in the annual field-day competitions. I looked upon these events as my opportunities to shine, and I felt proud whenever I won a little medal or a ribbon for my accomplishments. I also liked my classmates, many of whom I literally grew up with, and I would never have dreamed of leaving them to go to another school. Finally, I also looked up to my teachers—in spite of their frequent verbal abuse and liberal use of corporal punishment. After all, they were the only teachers that I had ever known, and I desperately wanted them to like me and to praise me the same way they liked and praised my sister. Unfortunately, however, I never received this kind of treatment from my teachers until I reached high school.

Becoming an Honor Student

My high school, although public, was very small. With fewer than 350 students in grades nine through twelve, it was dwarfed by the community's other high school which was more than four times larger. Even though my sister and I lived in the county school district and should therefore have attended the larger county school, our parents opted to pay tuition in order to send us both to the smaller city school.[6] They did so primarily because most of our friends were attending the city school, but they also liked the idea of having us go to a small school. Having both attended a very large high school in Southwestern Ohio with an enrollment of more than 4000 students, our parents believed that the educational advantages of attending a large school—wider course offerings, additional extracurricular activities, and greater resources in general— were far outweighed by the everyday challenges of trying to negotiate a sprawling building, layers of administrators, impersonal teachers, and masses of students.

My life as a student changed abruptly when I entered this high school. Finding myself in a new setting, surrounded by new teachers and new classmates—few of whom knew me as an underachiever—I realized that this was my one big chance to become a good student if I really wanted to. I remember being scared at first, scared that I would not succeed. My old teachers had always said that I was capable, but what if they were wrong? What if I were to try as hard as I could and not succeed? What if I were simply not smart enough? I remember having these thoughts during the first few weeks of school. Then I received my first report card— all *A*s and *B*s. I could hardly believe it; I had actually made the Honor Roll! A few days later, my name appeared in the local newspaper alongside everyone else who had made the Honor Roll, including my sister, and that night I received a phone call from the "headmistress" of my old school. Having seen my name listed in the newspaper, she called to offer me her congratulations. I still remember how proud I felt listening to her voice over the telephone. After years of being yelled at, threatened, and sometimes hit by this teacher for not working to my potential, I finally received the kind of positive attention that I had so often longed for.

After making the Honor Roll as a ninth-grader, my confidence grew, and I continued to excel academically in each successive year. It was as if I had finally discovered the secret formula for success that my sister had mastered so many years before: work hard, study hard, be passive, and do everything that the teachers said. It all seemed so simple—and it worked too. By the time I reached the twelfth grade, I actually joined my sister in being inducted into the National Honor Society, an achievement which I viewed at the time as representing the pinnacle of academic success. To me, becoming a member of this group meant that I had truly "made it" as a student.

Biology and Track

My favorite subject in high school was biology. I liked the order and the structure of the various systems of classification; I liked the hands-on aspect of studying specimens and doing dissections; and I liked the idea of being a scientist—just like when I was a child and dreamed of becoming an astronaut. I also liked the teacher. Similar to my elementary teachers in both personality and temperament, she was an older woman in her late sixties who had been teaching for more than 30 years. Unlike my past teachers, however, she did not yell at me. Instead, she actually seemed to like me. I worked hard to win her approval—to prove that I was a good student—and in return, she showed me a degree of respect that I had never before experienced from a teacher. When I was a sophomore, she chose me to represent the entire school in a statewide science and math competition. This event marked the beginning of a special relationship between me and her, for although I did well in all of my subjects, I began to put an extra effort into biology—and I started to think about pursuing it as a career.

In addition to this teacher, I was also greatly influenced by my track coach, a young science teacher who had been an All-American football player in college. His demeanor was loud, domineering, and authoritarian—the exact opposite of mine—but he genuinely cared about those whom he coached, and he motivated me to do my best. Weighing nearly 300 pounds, he struck an imposing figure. "You'll do it *my* way or hit the *high*-way!" he used to shout at the start of each new season, his deep voice always booming several decibels louder than the situation required. Then, he would glare at us in order to heighten the effect. Predictably, the younger team members were afraid of him, but we older athletes just sat there and secretly smiled, for we knew that he was really both fair and considerate, and we knew that the younger athletes would soon see through his bluster.

Following the same formula that had worked so well for me in the classroom—trying hard and doing everything that was asked of me—I thrived under my coach's direction, and he regularly held me up as a role model for the other runners. "Do you see what you can accomplish with a lot of hard work and dedication?" he would ask them. "All you have to do is look at Jimmy Muchmore!" I loved getting this kind of attention; it made me want to work that much harder.

In my last year of high school, I began to think about college with two goals in mind. First, I wanted to major in biology, and second, I wanted to continue to compete in the sport of track and field. Although I was uncertain about what career I would ultimately pursue, I felt that I definitely wanted to do something that would involve biology—perhaps be a forest ranger, or a naturalist, or a veterinarian, or even a medical doctor; the list went on. Like many young people, I was idealistic, and I wanted to do something that would help people and make a positive difference in the world.

My second goal was a bit more self-centered. At the Kentucky State High School Track and Field Championships, where I competed during my senior year, my high school coach introduced me to the track coach at Western Kentucky University, an institution that had a very strong reputation in athletics.[7] This particular coach had helped to develop several Olympic-caliber runners from around the world, and, although he usually recruited heavily from overseas, he was now looking for a few local athletes to fill out his roster. His personality was dynamic, and his talk was inspiring. He said that I had the potential to be a good middle distance runner and that he would like to coach me—not as a scholarship athlete, but as a "walk-on." A scholarship, he said, might come later if I continued to improve.

I did not care about not being offered a scholarship. To me, the important thing was the fact that this coach believed in me and felt that I had potential. I desperately wanted to run track in college, and this opportunity seemed like a dream-come-true. I remember visiting the campus with my father and my high school coach and being shown around by the college coach. Finishing the tour in the coach's office beneath the stadium, I stared up at the rows of photographs that covered the walls. They were pictures of alumni who had gone on to greater things. Most of them were All-Americans, while a few had actually competed in the Olympic Games. I was in awe, sitting there staring at these pictures, and I began to daydream about what it would be like to go to this university. I imagined myself training there, and perhaps one day becoming an All-American or even going to the Olympics myself. I imagined my own picture hanging on the coach's wall—another addition to his impressive collection. My mind was still swirling with these thoughts when the coach suddenly brought me back to earth with a question.

"So, do you think you'll be joining us in the fall?"

"What? Uhm… Yes," I said, still intoxicated by the pictures on the wall. I made my decision—just like that. I was going to Western Kentucky University.

During the summer months that followed, before moving away from home, I continued to think about all that lay ahead and was anxious for this next phase of my life to begin. Soon after I arrived on the campus, however, all of my hopes and dreams were suddenly dashed. The coach who had recruited me abruptly resigned to go to another university, and a new coach took his place. This new coach was very different. Cold and unemotional, he completely ignored the younger non-scholarship runners like me and chose instead to spend all of his time working with a small group of elite athletes on the team. I went to practice every day, week after week, hoping to prove to this man that I was worthy of his attention. But, week after week, he routinely ignored me—never offering a word of encouragement and seldom even acknowledging that I existed.

Needless to say, I was extremely disappointed, and I soon began to regret my decision to attend Western Kentucky. Not only was my experience on the track team a disappointing one, but college life in general was not what I had expected. In high school, I had become a very serious student, and I had expected to be surrounded by equally serious students in college. I was not prepared for the "party" atmosphere that prevailed—with students regularly skipping classes, seldom studying, and getting drunk on the weekends. Living on the seventeenth floor of a massive twenty-five-floor dormitory for men, I found it increasingly difficult to study. I had never dreamed that college students would be so nonchalant about their schoolwork. I was also disappointed with my biology courses, which no longer excited me like they had in the past. Clearly, it had been the teacher and not the content that had drawn me to this subject in high school, and I now began to question, more than ever, exactly what I wanted to do with my life. In addition, I was homesick. Never having been away from my family for such an extended period of time, I missed my parents, and I missed my grandparents. I even missed my sister.

Transferring to Vanderbilt

During the early spring of my freshman year, I happened to visit my sister at Vanderbilt University in Nashville, Tennessee, where she was then a student. When I mentioned how unhappy I was, she surprised me by saying, "Well, why don't you transfer here?"

"Transfer?" I thought. "Transfer to Vanderbilt?" Her question took me aback. I had always thought of Vanderbilt as my sister's university— *her* domain—and I believed that it was much too rigorous and too prestigious of a school for me to even think about attending. It had a strong academic reputation, and although I had done nearly as well as my sister in high school, I still had lingering doubts about my ability as a student. I simply did not consider myself to be at her level, and I was intimidated by the thought of going to a school that arrogantly called itself "The Harvard of the South." Yet when my sister suggested that I transfer, I suddenly saw things in a different light. Obtaining her approval had always been important to me, and now, implicit in her suggestion, was her belief that I was indeed capable of succeeding at Vanderbilt. She had seldom before expressed this kind of confidence in me, and I felt invigorated. "Of course!" I thought. "Why couldn't I transfer?" After all, I had scored fairly well on my college entrance examination, and I had a good grade-point-average at Western Kentucky. Maybe I *could* transfer to Vanderbilt.

However, there were two things that worried me. First, the tuition at Vanderbilt was very high—nearly ten times the tuition at Western Kentucky—and I knew that my parents were already financially strapped with the cost of my sister's education. They were not wealthy by any means. Second, it was already early April, and I was afraid that the deadline for submitting applications for the fall term had already passed. Fortunately, my parents were extremely supportive, saying that if I really wanted to transfer to Vanderbilt, then I should not worry about the money. They promised to help me in every way that they could, just like they were helping my sister. My parents made great sacrifices for both of us, and with the help of government loans, we were eventually able to come up with the money.

In dealing with the second problem, the deadline, I decided to contact the track coach at Vanderbilt and seek his advice. Coincidentally, the Western Kentucky Track Team just happened to be competing at Vanderbilt that weekend, so I took advantage of this opportunity to introduce myself. Waiting for a lull in the meet, I approached the Vanderbilt coach and explained my situation. He was a nice man, very laid-back and friendly, and he seemed interested in what I had to say.

"What's your major?" he asked.

"Biology," I said.

"Oh, that's too bad," he replied, with a look of disappointment on his face. "Biology is in the College of Arts and Sciences, and their deadline for applications was back in February...." The rest of his words trailed off, as my heart sunk. All I could think was that I would now have to wait another full year before I could transfer, and I dreaded having to go back to Western Kentucky. Then, I heard him say, "...however, you can still get into Peabody. Their deadline isn't until June."

"Really?" I replied. "But I don't think I want to be a teacher." I had heard about Peabody, Vanderbilt's College of Education, and most of it was disparaging. Although I later learned that Peabody College was considered by many educators to be one the top teachers' colleges in the United States, especially in the field of special education, all I knew at the time was that Peabody students were generally looked down upon by the rest of the Vanderbilt community. From talking to my sister and her friends, I knew that Peabody was considered to be an easy college which offered easy classes to less capable students who wanted to go to Vanderbilt but did not have the academic credentials to get into the more selective College of Arts and Sciences.[8] I was also aware of the relatively low status of teaching as a profession, and I completely agreed with the widely-held perception that only mediocre students became teachers. Strange as it may sound, I felt that I had worked too hard to establish myself as a good student to waste it all by becoming a teacher.

"But you wouldn't have to become a teacher," the coach said. "Once you get accepted into Peabody, you could then transfer to the College of Arts and Sciences and change your major back to biology. It would be like coming into the University through the back door. Lots of people do it this way.... Of course, you shouldn't tell the people at Peabody. They probably wouldn't like the idea of their college being used as a loophole."

During the next couple of days, I thought a great deal about what the coach had said. Should I attempt to transfer to Vanderbilt by declaring education as my major, even though I did not really want to become a teacher, or should I wait another year and attempt to transfer directly into the College of Arts and Sciences? I was very confused and did not know what to do. Although my natural inclination was to do it the "right way" and not try to "sneak in" through the back door, I was so unhappy at Western Kentucky that I simply could not bear the thought of waiting another year. So, as a nineteen-year-old, I made a decision that I am some-what embarrassed about today. I followed the coach's advice and applied to Peabody with no real intention of becoming a teacher. I felt very guilty about having done this—so guilty, in fact, that I ultimately decided not to change my major back to biology. Instead, I stayed in Peabody, and my opinion about teaching gradually changed.

CHAPTER 2

BECOMING A TEACHER

I liked the atmosphere at Vanderbilt—or at least certain aspects of it. I liked the ivy-covered buildings, the rolling lawns, and the cobblestone walkways, all of which lent an air of classic beauty to the campus. I also liked the seriousness and dedication with which most of the students approached their schoolwork. It was very different from the "party" atmosphere I had experienced at Western Kentucky. One thing that I did not like, however, was the conspicuous wealth and political conservatism that dominated the campus. *The Fiske Guide to Colleges* (Fiske, 1988) describes Vanderbilt students as "a mixture and overlap of Republicans, fraternity and sorority siblings, and 'Bible-thumping Presbyterians.'" Continuing, it states, "Indeed, this is a rather homogeneous bunch of students. About 92% are white and many are wealthy Southern preppies from the exclusive schools of Atlanta, Memphis, Dallas, and Virginia..." (p. 681).

Coming from a family of decidedly modest means and being much more liberal than conservative in my political orientation, I never felt entirely at ease in this setting—and the fact that I was a Peabody student often made me feel even more out of place. At a university where money and wealth were so important, the goal of becoming a teacher was not held in high esteem. Whenever I met other students for the first time, and the conversation inevitably turned toward the question, "What school are you in?" I dreaded having to say "Peabody."

"Oh?" they would respond—sometimes with a touch of disdain in their voices, and other times with hint of condescension. In both cases, the subtle message was the same: "Why are you in Peabody? Don't you know that you'll never make any money as a teacher. You must be awfully dumb not to have been able to get into Arts and Sciences."

Initially, I also had a difficult time fitting in on the track team. Most of my teammates were engineering students, and they spent a great deal of time discussing the difficulty of their courses. Materials Science, Physical Chemistry, Heat Transfer—even the names sounded imposing. In contrast, I was the lone Peabody student on the team, and my courses had such light-hearted names as Introduction to Exceptionality, Math for Elementary Teachers, and Language Arts in Elementary Schools. To my teammates, these courses sounded incredibly easy, and, although they never said it outright, I often sensed that they did not respect what I did. Nevertheless, I stayed in Peabody and gradually shaped my identity around the idea of being a teacher. After a while, the slights no longer bothered me, and I actually began to take pride in the fact that I had chosen a career path in which I might actually help people instead of simply making money.

I chose Special Education as my major because it was reputed to be the most difficult major that Peabody offered. I wanted my course of study to be as challenging as possible. "If I am going to be a Peabody student," I remember thinking, "then I at least want the most rigorous major available." I initially felt that having this major might help to elevate my status somewhat within the Vanderbilt community, but that was not the only reason. I was also genuinely interested in helping students with special needs. Feeling that I had been treated badly and misunderstood by most of my elementary teachers, I welcomed the opportunity to make up for some of these wrongs. And what better way, I thought, than to dedicate my life to helping students with physical and/or mental challenges? I suppose I saw myself rescuing children—much like Holden Caulfield in *The Catcher in the Rye* (Salinger, 1951). In one memorable passage, Holden says:

> ...I keep picturing these little kids playing some game in this big field of rye and all. Thousands of little kids, and nobody's around—nobody big, I mean—except me. And I'm standing on the edge of some crazy cliff. What I have to do, I have to catch everybody if they start going over the cliff—I mean if they're running and they don't look where they're going I have to come out from somewhere and catch them. That's all I'd do all day. I'd just be the catcher in the rye... (p. 173).

It was a romantic notion—the idea that I would save children from the kinds of experiences that I had had as a student—yet, nothing that I encountered in my education courses ever caused me to expand this simplistic view. Only once was I ever asked to reflect in writing on why I wanted to become a teacher, and then it was only a minor exercise. I wrote the following brief paragraph:

I would like to work in education because I love children. Children are constantly growing and developing both mentally and physically, and it is exciting for me to think that I can help to direct this growth. Handicapped children in particular need a more specialized direction in order to reach their full potential. Quite simply, the learning process has always fascinated me, and I believe that it would be very personally satisfying to me to purse it as a career.

I was very sincere in what I wrote, even if it does sound trite and formulaic. I did enjoy working with children, and I was genuinely interested in the various theories that I was learning in my education classes. The problem was that I had never really thought about my reasons for becoming a teacher long enough or deeply enough to be able to write anything more sophisticated—and the assignment did not require me to do so. The professor responded with an equally brief and superficial notation. "Jim, thank you for sharing your thoughts and feelings with me. You have a great deal to offer the individuals you will work with and teach." As I recall, we then quickly moved on to the seemingly more important task of developing our technical competencies in the "science" of teaching.

The preservice teacher education curriculum at Peabody was very traditional in the early 1980s. In addition to the standard academic requirements—math, science, English, and history—I took education courses ranging from educational psychology, to classroom measurement and assessment, to speech and language development. I also took the usual teaching methods courses in reading, language arts, math, science, and social studies, all of which I needed to become certified in special education (grades K-12), and the elementary grades (1-8). I worked hard in my classes, earned good grades, and regularly made the Dean's List. Once, after a particularly good semester, I even received a personal letter of commendation from the Chair of the Special Education Department. It said the following:

> Dear Jim:
> I have recently received your transcript from the past semester. Congratulations on an outstanding performance. Your grades reflect your hard and diligent work. It's performance such as you have displayed in the last semester that predicts contributions to the field of Special Education. Have a nice summer, and I will see you in the fall.

I felt proud of my accomplishments, and, with the encouragement of the Chair, I was very excited about the idea of being a teacher. My undergraduate education culminated with a final rite of passage: student teaching. I had two placements, each lasting seven weeks. My first placement was in a self-contained special education classroom for students with severe and multiple handicaps. In order to qualify for this classroom, the students had to have at least two handicapping conditions. For example, they had to be emotionally disturbed *and* mentally retarded, or mentally retarded *and* autistic. My second placement was in a regular sixth-grade classroom in an urban middle school. The students were racially diverse—60 percent African-American and 40 percent Caucasian, with the white students being bused from an outlying suburb in order to comply with a court-ordered desegregation plan.

Having saved most of my notes, papers, and assignments from Peabody—all of them neatly organized and stored in a large filing cabinet—it is relatively easy for me to reconstruct my experiences as a preservice teacher. Opening the bottom drawer, for example, one of the first files that I encounter is labeled "Student Teaching Log." It contains a stapled packet of lined paper—approximately thirty sheets—each with a single handwritten entry. Leafing through these pages, I can relive for a moment my life as a student teacher.

> *Tuesday, March 6, 1984:* I was really overwhelmed and frustrated on my first day in my sixth-grade student teaching placement. The son of one of the teachers died in an accident over the weekend, and my cooperating teacher went to the funeral. It lasted all morning, and there was no substitute— just me. I was not expecting to assume this level of responsibility on my very first day, and my lack of familiarity with the students, the schedule, and the curriculum left me very confused for much of the day. I really had no idea what I was doing. In addition, after having been in a setting which consisted of eight young, very low-functioning autistic and severely emotionally disturbed children, today's experience with almost 70 regular sixth-graders came as somewhat of a shock. I expect to be able to adjust during the next few days, although it will definitely take some getting used to.

> *Monday, March 12, 1984:* Today, I taught fractions to two students who were performing at a level below the other chil-

dren in the class. I really enjoy working with students such as these because they are the ones who are truly needy. I feel that I have a lot to offer to them, and I am making a special effort to interact with those quiet students who sit back in the corner and usually get ignored.

Wednesday, March 14, 1984: I took over one of the math groups today. There are three math classes, and each class is currently divided into two groups. One group is working on decimals, while the other is working on fractions. I have taken a special interest in a student from one of the fraction groups. He sits in the corner and is very quiet. It would be very easy to ignore him. Today, I spent ten minutes explaining to him how to rename a fraction, and after using several concrete models, he finally caught on. I felt great! And he too was really excited that he understood.

Monday, March 19, 1984: I felt wonderful today. Everything seemed to go right, and I had absolutely no problems in anything! I implemented my own lesson plan for the first time, instead of following the teacher's, and it went very well. The students were interested, and by the end of the lesson, they all understood the concept that I was teaching. What a feeling! To teach something so that it is understood by someone who previously did not understand it is an incredible experience. Days like to today make life very pleasant!

Tuesday, April 17, 1984: Teaching all day is very tiring, and there is no time to recover afterwards because I must spend several hours preparing for the next day. I can understand how teachers can get burned out. Another difficulty that I have is managing materials and paperwork. To keep track of everything, I must always concentrate on the task at hand. Referring to my daily lesson plan is helpful, but going from one class to another with only five minutes to organize my thoughts makes me feel that I am always in a hurry.

Thursday, April 26, 1984: What a disaster! During the assembly today, I had a nightmare of an experience. To begin with, I was not feeling very well. I was tired and lethargic due to a lack of sleep, and when the students came back to homeroom after lunch to get ready to go to the assembly, they were very rowdy. They would not sit down and be quiet like they were supposed to, despite all of my efforts to get them to do so. I realize now that it was only about four students who were misbehaving, but at the time it seemed like it was the entire class. It is so easy to ignore the ones who are behaving. Well, to make a long story short, I overreacted and excluded the entire class from the assembly. This was a huge mistake! The students who were misbehaving did not care, while the ones who were innocent were furious. In an instant, I had the entire class against me. I thought the day would never end!

Friday, April 27, 1984: I was very apprehensive this morning. Yesterday's disaster was still vivid in my mind. When I arrived at school, however, I was relieved to find that everything seemed to be okay. The only reminder of yesterday came when I saw the four students who were the most abusive toward me. They would not even look at me. They knew that they had done wrong. All morning, I thought about what I should do—if anything—but as it turned out, the four students took the initiative. They voluntarily stayed inside during their Physical Education period, and then they apologized for the way that they had acted. It was a very touching moment. Later, in the afternoon, I gave the entire class one half-hour of playtime outside to make up for their missed assembly. At the end of the day, they all seemed to have forgotten about yesterday's incident, and they liked me again.[9]

In reading these entries, I see myself as a young, inexperienced, and very idealistic student teacher. I am particularly struck by the language that I used, which can provide an insight into some of the underlying assumptions that guided my actions. For example, in my March 14 entry, when I wrote about how good it felt to help a student learn a new math concept, the image is of a teacher swooping down to rescue a poor struggling student. First the student did not understand; then I taught him; then he understood. It is what I might call a "teacher as savior" theme. In another entry, on March 19, I wrote that I "implemented" a lesson, my word choice suggesting that I viewed my teaching role as delivering standardized, prepackaged components to the students. It represents a "teacher as technician" theme. In addition, implicit in most of my entries is a very teacher-centered view of the classroom. The way I saw it, everything was supposed to emanate from the teacher—which is not surprising since that was exactly how I had experienced school when I was a student. Opening another drawer, I see a file labeled Psychology 2310, Spring-1982. Inside are all of my class notes, two multiple choice exams, and a term paper entitled "Behaviorism and How it Relates to the Classroom Curriculum." In this paper, I briefly summarized the work of two well-known psychologists, John Watson and B. F. Skinner, and then showed how operant conditioning and reinforcement could be used in the classroom. I wrote:

> Using reinforcement, a teacher can control a student's behavior so that it meets the curriculum objectives of the class. For example, when a student completes an assignment which corresponds to the teacher's desired outcome, the teacher should perform some event such as the presentation of an *A* which will cause the frequency of the desired behavior to increase.

Today, I can hardly believe that I actually wrote these words. The idea of a teacher magically "controlling" a student's behavior and systematically shaping it toward "desired outcomes" by wielding letter grades sounds incredibly naive. It was probably this kind of thinking—with an emphasis on extrinsic rewards and punishments—that led me to exclude my class from the assembly during my student teaching.

The theory of behaviorism was central to the special education curriculum at Peabody, and it heavily influenced the way I viewed teaching and learning in schools. Leafing through another of my old folders—this one from my first student teaching placement—I see the final report that I wrote for a behavior modification project that I did with one of my students. In it I wrote the following:

> SB is an eleven-year-old boy who has been identified as being autistic, mildly retarded, emotionally disturbed, and language delayed. He is also easily distracted, and this distractibility seems to be directly related to his rate of completion of simple addition and subtraction problems. Consequently, the student teacher collected data concerning antecedents, behaviors, and consequences. This informal assessment device was constructed so that specific behavioral data could be collected and analyzed with the resulting analysis form-

ing the framework of a behavior intervention program. After examining the data, the student teacher determined that a reinforcement program which rewarded on-task behavior should be implemented. This program used edible reinforcers, the administration of which was contingent upon the number of problems completed during a given interval of time. After several trial runs which excluded the use of reinforcers, a completion criterion of two problems per minute (measured in six 5-minute intervals) was deemed appropriate....

The first thing that I notice about this passage is my writing style—so clinical, so objective, and so scientific. But that was how I had been taught. I was mimicking the style of writing that I had so often seen in my textbooks and coursepack articles, where the authors wrote in the third person and never said "I." My professors had encouraged me to write this way—systematically detaching myself from all of the events at hand and describing the situation from the perspective of a non-participant. First-person writing, they had stressed, was to be avoided at all times, even if it meant awkwardly referring to myself as "the student teacher."

The second thing that strikes me about this passage is the ridiculousness of the entire project—although I certainly did not consider it ridiculous at the time. Basically, what I did was give a boy a piece of candy whenever he completed 10 math problems in five minutes. On the first day, he completed five problems, eight problems, seven problems, and eight problems, before finally reaching the magic number of 10. Then, after receiving his first piece of candy the number shot to 40. "Wow!" I remember thinking, "this behaviorism stuff really works!"

During the next week, I continued to give the student a piece of candy whenever he completed at least 10 math problems in the given period of time, and he continued to exceed this threshold. "He really loves his candy," I thought. "Plus, he's learning math." Everything was going smoothly, until one day, while in the midst of one of his intervals, the student suddenly shouted, "Oh, my God!" Glancing up from my stopwatch, I saw an expression of horror etched on his face.

"What's the matter?" I asked. Had another student crawled under the table and grabbed his foot? Was he having a seizure? Had he witnessed a murder out the classroom window? What?

"Look!" he said, holding up his pencil for me to see. The lead was broken; that was all. His pencil had broken, and he had realized that the time it would take him to get up and sharpen it would cause him to miss his criterion and therefore miss his next piece of candy. What had I done to this poor student?

In retrospect, I believe that by thinking about his education solely in terms of antecedents, behaviors, and consequences, I had treated him more as a laboratory animal than as a person, and he had behaved accordingly. At the time, however, I attributed this incident more to my lack of experience than to any kind of fundamental problem with my approach. "When I learn how to operate a stopwatch more covertly and keep my tally sheet hidden, then the students won't be so nervous," I remember thinking.

Even in my general elementary methods classes, where the behaviorism of Watson and Skinner was overshadowed by the cognitive psychology of Jean Piaget, there was still an underlying assumption that teaching was systematic, scientific, and very technical. Looking through another one of my files, I see a packet of lesson plans that I created for a remedial reading practicum. For six weeks, I worked one-on-one with Jason, a second-grader who had been brought to the Peabody Reading Tutorial Program by his mother. She had been told by Jason's teacher that his reading skills were low and that he was probably going to be retained in the second grade if his skills did not improve. Following a procedure that had been outlined in my remedial reading methods class, I used the test-teach-test method of instruction. First, I identified his problems through a test. Then, I remediated these problems with a carefully designed intervention. Finally, I used another test to assess the outcome. The entire process was analogous to the way in which a doctor would diagnose and treat a disease.

I began by administering the *Gilmore Oral Reading Test* (Gilmore & Gilmore, 1968). The results indicated that Jason's oral reading accuracy was "above average," while his literal comprehension and rate of reading were "average." Next, I did a reading miscue analysis (Goodman, 1969), in which I systematically analyzed Jason's skills in decoding and comprehension. This test revealed that whenever Jason came to an unfamiliar word, he was usually able to sound it out using phonics, but that he seldom utilized context clues. Almost two-thirds of his miscues involved the substitution of words that served different grammatical functions, and these substitutions often changed the meaning of the passage. For example, he pronounced "greet" as "great" and "complete" as "company." In my initial diagnostic report, I also noted that he tended to read in a disinterested, monotone voice and that he seemed to be very nervous about being tested.

After completing the diagnostic testing, I designed a remedial program to address Jason's area of weakness. Twice a week, I met with him in Peabody's Kennedy Center and "implemented" a carefully-planned lesson. Remembering how boring my own reading instruction had been when I was in elementary school, I tried to make these lessons fun and exciting. I once wrote out instructions for him on how to make a paper airplane, which he had to read and follow. Another time, I designed and created a board game called "Race Car Driver" in which we both took turns reading cards and following directions. My rationale for doing these kinds of activities was to create situations for Jason where the consequence for "misreading" a word would be immediate and tangible. If he did not read the directions correctly, for example, then his paper airplane would not fly, or his race car would not make it to the finish line. In this way, I thought, the activities themselves would serve as powerful reinforcers for accurate reading.

At the end of the practicum, I administered another form of the *Gilmore Oral Reading Test.* This time, the results indicated that Jason was "above average" in all three areas—decoding, comprehension, and reading rate—and I remember thinking that I had done a great job. One year later, however, I encountered Jason's mother on a Nashville sidewalk.

"How's Jason doing?" I asked.

"Oh, not very well," she replied. "Do you know that he almost failed the second grade? The teacher said that he was just not doing his work. Now, he's just doing enough to get by in the third grade. I don't know what to do with him."

I think that Jason was a lot like me when I was a student. He was probably successful in the tutoring sessions because I had showed an interest in him as a person—just like my high school biology teacher had shown an interest in me. Although I instinctively knew that the personal dimension of teaching was important, it was many years before I figured out how to make it central to my classroom teaching. In the meantime, I continued to think about teaching primarily in terms of behavioral objectives, standardized procedures, and administering tests.

Earning a Master's Degree

After graduating from Vanderbilt in August, 1984, I decided to remain at Peabody College for another year in order to earn my master's degree in Reading Education. I was particularly intrigued by the history of this field and the way that researchers through the years had used the scientific method to systematically study and analyze the reading process. Moving from the classic eye-movement studies by Javel (1879), Dodge (1907) and Buswell (1922), to the seminal comprehension research of Thorndike (1917), Pearson (1974), and Anderson (1977), to the elaborate model-building by Holmes (1953), Gough (1976), and Goodman (1976), I spent hours in the Peabody Education Library, merrily browsing through the stacks and exploring their large collection of old books and journals.

The Holmes (1953) article was one of my favorites. It was entitled "Basic Assumptions Underlying the Substrata-Factor Theory." Working from the assumption that the ability to read was dependent upon the interaction of a collection of organized neurological subsystems, Holmes identified some 80 variables that he felt were related to reading success. Then, using statistical techniques to identify those that had the largest effects, he constructed an elaborate three-dimensional diagram to illustrate his findings. I liked this article not necessarily because of the content but simply because it sounded so technical and scientific—just like I thought research was supposed to be.

Returning to my filing cabinet, I again use my class notes and papers to reconstruct my thinking—this time as a graduate student. In one of my folders, for example, I see an assignment that consisted of going to the library and picking out five journal articles to summarize and critique. Today, I have only the faintest recollection of actually doing this assignment, yet what I wrote provides a good insight into the way that I was viewing research. In response to an article entitled "A Method for Teaching Sight Words to Disabled Readers" (McNinch, 1981), I wrote the following critique:

> The article is very straight-forward and pragmatic. The author's step-by-step description of the strategy is logically ordered and internally consistent. However, his evaluation of its effectiveness is based solely upon teacher reports and testimonials, not upon scientific data. There should be objec-

tive research implemented so that the strategy's strengths and
weaknesses can be determined.

In another critique—this one of Bradley's (1981) article called "A Tactile
Approach to Reading"—I was even more dismissive of non-scientific
approaches. I wrote:

> This article provides an affirmative testimonial concerning
> the effectiveness of a tactile approach to reading, but the au-
> thor provides no real data to support her view. Instead, she
> simply uses three case studies to laud her particular approach,
> and there is no real substance to back up her claims. As a
> result, her conclusions should be interpreted as personal con-
> jecture rather than as objective facts.

The standard by which I judged good research was deeply rooted in
the assumptions of mainstream quantitative social science. I believed that
just because a teacher tried something and found that it worked did not
mean that it should be readily embraced by other teachers—any more
than a physician's anecdotal reports of a particular medical treatment
should be readily accepted by other medical doctors. There first had to be
"scientific" evidence. I probably developed this attitude partly from my
own background in science and partly from the influence of my professors. One professor, in particular, often spoke disparagingly of teachers
who did not base their practices upon what he considered to be sound
educational research. Bad teachers, he felt, were those who ignored scientific research or implemented it poorly.

In spite of my feelings about what counted as legitimate educational
research, my perspective on reading was surprisingly holistic. The Holmes
model notwithstanding, I think I was always skeptical of a reductionistic
perspective in which reading was considered to be a set of discrete
subskills—such as spelling, comprehension, vocabulary, and decoding—
that could be taught in isolation. Perhaps I remembered the boring workbook pages and ditto sheets that I had been forced to complete when I
was in elementary school. Or maybe I simply saw how ineffective such
approaches were when I was a preservice teacher. Whatever the reason,
when I was asked to define "reading" on the take-home portion of a final
exam, I defined it not as a collection of separate and distinct skills, but as
"an interactive process through which individuals construct meaning from

print." Later, in this same paper, I wrote, "I view reading as a holistic process which cannot effectively be broken down into a series of subskills; it is much too complex of an interaction between the reader and the text." Reading, I felt, was much more than the sum of its component parts.

Anxious to receive a good grade, however, I was careful not to dismiss a skills-based approach entirely. I knew that the professor would probably disapprove of my stance, so I continued my essay by writing:

> There is usually a high positive correlation between the mastery of certain skills and fluent reading. Reading tests can measure these skills, but there are certain aspects of reading that cannot be measured. No test can measure the specific processes that occur during reading. The interpreter of a test can only make inferences about the process. No test can measure reading in its natural state—that of a holistic process. But if the interpreter of a test is competent, then the inferences that are made can be quite accurate.

My argument closely followed the position that I had inferred from my professor—that although reading instruction was not a precise science it was close, and that any shortcomings of a skills approach were probably the result of incompetent teaching, rather than the approach itself.

In fact, I believed that the best way to teach a child to read was not through skills-driven basal readers and isolated phonics instruction, but rather through continued exposure to a literate environment—the same way that my sister and I had learned to read. Intuitively, I felt that it was the teacher's job to set up this environment, stocking the classroom with real books, reading to the children, and providing them with significant opportunities to read and discuss books. My views were somewhat consistent with what later came to be known as whole language. At that time, however, this term was not yet familiar to me, and with no support from the research literature or encouragement from my professors, I did not attempt to develop a pedagogy that was consistent with this philosophy. Instead, I dutifully embraced the ideas of my professors, thinking that they knew best. After all, I thought, they were the experts.

Today, I see two shortcomings in the way that reading was conceived and taught by my professors at Peabody College. First, they paid absolutely no attention to writing. Looking through several of my old course syllabi, I see class sessions on topics ranging from "word attack," to "reading comprehension," to "developmental reading," to "reading disability," but I see no mention of the term "writing." Indeed, the only time that writing was ever discussed in any of my classes was in the context of handwriting and penmanship. Important questions, such as "How do children learn to write?", "How can writing be evaluated?", and "How can teachers help students to improve their writing?", were never addressed. Instead, there was always an implicit assumption that writing was an innate talent that some people had a flair for and other people did not—and that there was nothing a teacher could do to change it. As a result, I left Peabody with very little sense of how to teach students to write, other than engaging in the time-worn practice of assigning students topics and then marking their "mistakes" with a red pen.

The second thing that was missing was a recognition of the social and political dimensions of literacy. The entire emphasis was on the psychology of reading, with absolutely no consideration given to the roles and the purposes that reading and writing serve in society. What is literacy? Why do people read and write? How does literacy help to establish and maintain social relationships? I later learned that these and other important questions were being addressed by scholars such as Greene (1982), Heath (1980, 1983), Smith (1983), Bloome (1985), Bloome and Green (1984), and Harste, Woodward and Burke (1984), but these works never appeared in any of my coursepacks or other required readings.

I remember sitting in class one time and listening to the professor lecture on the importance of getting children to read. "Reading is very important," he said, "and we want our students to read as much as possible." I remember thinking, "Yes, but *why* do we want children to read? *Why* is reading important?" At the time, however, these questions seemed too radical, and I did not ask them out of a fear that the professor would not take me seriously. I could just imagine him saying, "What do you mean? Don't you agree that reading is important?" It was easy for me to avoid pursuing these kinds of questions when I was at Peabody, but after I began to teach they were questions that I had to face every day. Why is reading important? Why should children learn to read?

Revisiting Joyce and
Exploring the Meaning of Literacy

Working with Joyce and the other students in my special education classroom in rural Kentucky was very difficult, yet I tried hard to be the best teacher that I could be. My strategy for Joyce involved a language experience approach (Hall, 1981). Since she was always eager to tell stories, I thought that transforming her words into print might be a good starting point. Not only would the text then have a strong personal meaning for her, but she would also be presented with a direct connection between spoken and written words. I hoped that she would internalize this connection and that it might be an event that would begin her on the road to fluent reading. I also had her start a word bank based on words she had come to know through her stories, and I used a few commercialized materials such as phonics workbooks and language kits, which were activities that I felt the principal and the other teachers expected me to use.

Throughout my year with Joyce, I found myself on a vicious "roller coaster ride." Days of encouraging progress were followed by weeks of disheartening setbacks, with the end result being that Joyce did *not* learn how to read. Although she *did* learn a few new sight words, and she *did* learn how to sign her name in cursive, on the whole, her reading skills were essentially no better in June than they were in October. I could not help but feel that I had failed her. I had tried everything that I knew and nothing had worked. Something was missing. Once, in one of her calmer moods, Joyce had asked me a very poignant question. "Why should I learn how to read? My daddy don't know how to read, and he gots a good job." I was taken aback by this question and at first did not know what to say.

"What does your daddy do?" I finally asked.

"He pumps gas at the truck stop," she replied with a trace of pride in her voice.

It was several years later, when I was a doctoral student at the University of Michigan, that I finally encountered a perspective on literacy that addressed Joyce's question. It began with my reading of Szwed (1981), who proposed that we examine the roles played by literacy in the lives of individuals—including the varieties of reading and writing available, the contexts for their use, and the manner in which they are perceived by those who use them. Then, I discovered that these topics had indeed been the focus of several ethnographic studies of literacy—studies which were very different from the kind of research that I had encountered at Peabody. For example, Fishman (1987, 1988) described the way that reading and writing were perceived and used by the children in an Old Order Amish family, while Wells (1986) conducted an extensive longitudinal study of the language and literacy of mainstream British children. Recording the children's development from early childhood through their entry into school, Wells chronicled their attempts to create meaning in their lives through language, and he showed that collaboration with a sympathetic community of adults was an important element in this natural endeavor.

In studying the lives of three adult readers in rural and coastal Nova Scotia, Neilsen (1989) found that although their reading and writing behaviors were quite different, they had all developed through a similar process. Each individual had become literate by responding to the events and contexts of their lives and accepting the values and expectations of their communities. Neilsen emphasized that school was only one of the contexts which influenced literacy, and she proposed that it was not necessarily a crucial one. For the individuals she studied, literacy was simply the outcome of a continuing process through which they had come to understand their worlds. Taylor (1983) drew similar conclusions in a study of young children's literacy development, reporting that "literacy enables (children) to participate fully in the social system of which they are a part" (p. 89).

In another qualitative study, Heath (1983) researched three communities in rural North Carolina and contrasted the language development of the children in each community. She observed substantial differences in the ways that language was perceived and used by adults in each community, and she noted a dichotomy between home and school uses of literacy. For example, several important uses of reading and writing were identified in the black working-class community of Trackton, but a discontinuity arose when these kinds of literacy were not equally valued in school. Heath (1983) states,

> Trackton children have learned through their long hours in the laps of adults and on the hard church benches, that in the free flow of time, there are multiple types of talk and song about the written word.... [Yet] Trackton students often drift through the school, hoping to escape with the valued piece of paper which they know will add much to their parents' and grandparents' pride, although little to their paychecks (p. 349).

Taylor and Dorsey-Gaines (1988) described a similar situation in their ethnographic study of several low-income, urban, African-American families. They concluded that being literate is a uniquely human experience that enables us to better understand ourselves and one another, but they also saw a discontinuity between literacy at home and literacy at school. They noted that it was possible for children to grow up literate but fail in school because educators expect them to excel only on narrowly defined tasks. At the same time, they pointed out that children are typically given little or no credit for their abilities to master the complex communicative process that is essential for success in everyday life. Griffin (1977) made a similar observation in her study of classroom literacy when she suggested that reading be viewed not as a discrete set of skills or concepts, but as a tool. Just as a carpenter uses tools to construct furniture, so too do readers and writers use literacy to construct meaning in their lives.

So what is literacy? Although Stubbs (1980) describes some of the problems associated with accepting a universal definition, I noticed a common theme running throughout each of the previously mentioned studies. Each researcher came to view literacy as the creation of meaning through a mastery of spoken and written language in relevant contexts. The term "context" is important here, because as Wagner (1986) observes, what counts as literacy in one context may not count as literacy in another. For example, a person usually thought of as being highly literate may not be able to understand the complex "legalese" of an insurance policy, or an "illiterate" Amish farmer with a limited understanding of reading and writing conventions may be regarded as highly literate in his community. During my first year as a doctoral student at the University of Michigan in 1990, I realized for the first time that literacy and illiteracy were dynamic terms whose meanings depended largely upon the contexts in which they were embedded. Greene (1982) states that "to achieve literacy is, in part, to learn how to think conceptually, to structure experience, to look through wider and more diverse perspectives at the lived world" (p. 85). As a result, like Cook-Gumperz (1986), I came to view literacy as the ability to create and understand spoken and written language as accepted in a community as well as all the changes this ability causes in the lives of those who participate in it.

From this perspective, I realized that Joyce actually had a very effective repertoire of literate behaviors that she used in the context of her home. For example, when she misrepresented my note to her father, she demonstrated that she understood the power of the written word. By presenting the note as a positive statement from her teacher, she used the power of the text to avoid a punishment and perhaps even to receive praise.

However, because she was unable to create and understand printed messages in the way that was accepted by the school, she was not fully literate in the sense that was implied by my definition of literacy.

Maxine Greene (1990) has stated that every child has a story to tell and that we should listen. When I worked with Joyce, she told many stories, but I was unwilling to listen to the ones that were important to her. Instead, I provided elaborate prompts to elicit fanciful language experience stories about the world as I saw it—not as Joyce had experienced it. In this way, I was depriving her of a true language experience. I suppose that I subconsciously feared what I might have learned had I probed too deeply into her life, and I never let her tell the stories that she wanted and needed to tell.

By reflecting on my experience with Joyce, I learned that literacy is more than just the technical skills necessary for reading and writing. It is also the changes that occur in one's life when these skills are used to develop a critical self-awareness (see, e.g., Freire & Macedo, 1987; Giroux, 1988; Greene, 1982; Philion, 1998; Willinsky, 2001). In retrospect, I wish I had allowed Joyce to tell the stories that had meaning for her. I wish I had let her tell stories about her father, her family, and her life. I wish I had permitted her to explore the meaning in her life through language—for I now believe that this approach may have enabled her to enter the mainstream world of textual literacy.

Teaching and Coaching in Ohio

I left my job in Kentucky at the end of that school year, thoroughly exhausted by my experiences. Teaching special education had been much more difficult than I had ever imagined, and I felt drained—both physically and emotionally. I remember asking myself, "What is it that I really want to do? Is it teaching or is it something else?" I had always liked history, and having worked for the Kentucky Historical Society for several summers during high school and college, I decided to apply for a full-time position there. Similarly, drawing upon my involvement in sports, I applied for the position of Head Track Coach at a small college in Illinois. In addition, since my father worked in state government, I thought about following in his footsteps and working for a government agency somewhere in Kentucky or Tennessee. I applied for several jobs in a variety of fields. In the end, however, I felt that I had invested too much of my life in becoming a teacher to quit after only one year, so I decided to try another teaching job.

After several weeks of job-searching, I was eventually hired to teach eighth-grade English and developmental reading in a suburban school district in Southwestern Ohio. They also wanted me to coach track and cross country at the high school level. I grew to love this job, especially the coaching part. During the three years that I worked there, I had the opportunity to coach several excellent athletes, including one who earned All-American status by finishing second at the National High School Cross Country Championships held in San Diego, California.

As a coach, I had a great deal of autonomy in designing workouts, and I enjoyed working with students in the less formal atmosphere of athletics. My teaching, on the other hand, was much more closely monitored, and it was often guided by curricular mandates and administrative edicts with which I strongly disagreed yet felt compelled to follow nonetheless. For example, the district-wide reading curriculum was based on a mastery learning system that was administered from the Central Office. The school district's Director of Instruction had put together lists of skills that were supposed to be taught at each grade level. Each skill was accompanied by a "pupil performance objective" stated in behavioral terms—such as "Given several passages, the student will correctly identify cause and effect relationships with 80 percent accuracy." The students' mastery of these skills was then assessed through a series of brief, five-item multiple choice tests.

The way this system worked in practice was as follows. First, the teacher would administer a pre-test in order to see how many students already knew the "skill of the day" (e.g., cause and effect, literal comprehension, main ideas, use of commas, etc.). Next, he or she would teach the skill using lectures, ditto sheets, or any other means that might be deemed appropriate. Then, after determining that all the students were ready, the teacher would administer a five-item, multiple choice post-test, that would be sent to the Central Office and scored by a computer. A printout of the results would later be returned to the teacher, revealing which students had met the mastery criterion. The entire process was recursive, meaning that the teacher was supposed to repeat it as many times as necessary until all of the students had mastered the required skill.

To the Director of Instruction at the Central Office, this approach probably made a great deal of sense. By specifying exactly what every teacher in the school district should teach, it ensured that all of the students would receive the same instruction, which would mean, at least in theory, that they would all have mastered the same skills—and more importantly, that they would all be well-primed for the district-wide standardized achievement test. To the Director of Instruction, mastery learning must have seemed like a great idea. In practice, however, it was fraught with some serious problems. First, the teaching of skills tended to take the place of authentic reading and writing. With a new skill to cover each week, as well as an ever-mounting collection of old skills that needed to be retaught, there was little time for teachers to do anything else. So time-consuming were these skills lessons, in fact, that the students seldom had time to participate in the very activity that they were supposed to be learning—reading. In my mind, this situation was analogous to a track coach trying to teach an athlete how to master the high jump without ever allowing him or her to experience the thrill of jumping over the crossbar and landing in the foam pit.

Another problem was that by treating reading as a collection of individual skills, instead of as a dynamic, interactive, and purposeful act, it made reading a very tedious subject. I remember one student having difficulty with the test on "following directions." He was a good student— one of the best readers in the class—but he missed two of the five items and therefore had to retake the test. He was embarrassed. After reteaching the skill, I felt confident that he would pass the test easily. Much to my surprise, however, he did not pass, but instead missed three items. He could not understand what he had done wrong. The next time, he missed four items, and then he missed all five. By now, he was so confused and frustrated that I could no longer work with him. He simply would not listen as I tried to teach him the skill for the fifth time. What had happened? The Director of Instruction would probably have said that I was not a good teacher and that I had done a poor job in teaching the skill. That may have been true, but there was also another explanation. Here was a student who already knew how to read, yet he was being penalized for not being able to pass a test on a skill that was supposed to be a vital component of reading. To me, the situation was so ridiculous that it was comical—but neither the student nor I was laughing.

Many times, I thought about simply ignoring these silly little tests and teaching reading in a way that was more consistent with my underlying beliefs about literacy—but I was much too scared to actually do it.

Another teacher at one of the elementary schools had been fired for disregarding the mandated reading program, and the Director of Instruction always kept a close watch on us teachers to make sure that we were in compliance. Having us send the students' test sheets to the Central Office for scoring was one of the ways that we were monitored. Of course, I probably could have filled in all of the students' test sheets with the correct answers myself and then dutifully sent them into the Central Office to be scored, but I simply did not have the nerve. "What if she visits my classroom?" I thought. "Or what if my students talk to other students and the word somehow gets back to her that I am not using the mandated curriculum?" Not wanting to live in a constant state of fear, I did what was required of me—even though it was diametrically opposed to my most fundamental beliefs about literacy.

Not everything was frustrating about this job, however. I had many positive moments, such as my unit on Anne Frank. Because *The Diary of Anne Frank*, a play written by Goodrich and Hackett (1956), was part of the eighth-grade English curriculum—and not the skills-based reading program—I had a great deal of freedom in deciding how it would be taught. At first, it was simply going to be a week-long unit. I figured I would begin by providing a bit of background information about World War II and the Holocaust, followed by our reading and discussion of the play, and perhaps culminating with our viewing of the movie version of the *Diary* starring Millie Perkins (Stevens, 1959). However, what started out as a simple little unit quickly mushroomed into a six-week mega-unit on Anne Frank that thoroughly engrossed both me and the students.

What made this unit so successful was the fact that it emerged spontaneously from our natural interest in the life of Anne Frank. Although I had heard of Anne Frank and knew who she was, I had never actually read her diary or seen the movie—so I began the unit with a sort of vague curiosity. Why had Anne become so famous? What was it about her diary that had captivated so many people? Just as I was starting to read the play, I happened to see an article in the local newspaper announcing the arrival of a traveling photographic exhibition on the life of Anne Frank. Organized by the Anne Frank House in Amsterdam and presented by the Greater Cincinnati Interfaith Holocaust Foundation and the University of Cincinnati (*Anne Frank in the world: 1929-1945*, 1987), the exhibition included more than 800 photographs, many of them previously unpublished family photos taken by Anne's father who was an amateur photographer. I went to the exhibition and was moved by what I saw. Many of the photographs had been processed onto silk screens and placed on giant polyurethane panels that were illuminated through backlighting, which gave them a haunting, lifelike quality. "If only my students could see this," I thought. Unfortunately, they could not. It was too late to arrange a field trip, so I did the next best thing. Going home and getting my 35mm camera, I came back and took pictures of some of the panels and created a slide show to present to my students. They were as intrigued as I was, and they immediately wanted to know more about Anne—how she had lived and why she had died.

During the next several weeks, my students and I became completely immersed in the life of Anne Frank, not only reading the play, but also studying World War II and the Holocaust. For example, after the success of my slide show, I showed my students a film called *Night and Fog* (Resnais, 1955), and then one of the students brought in a videotape on the Holocaust that he had recorded from his television at home. We also read some of Anne's other writing (Frank, 1983), as well as excerpts from the autobiography of Miep Gies (Gies with Gold, 1987), one of the women who had assisted the Frank family in hiding. Each day, it was something new—a different perspective on Anne Frank's life. The unit finally culminated with a series of student projects, ranging from reports on historical figures involved in the Holocaust, to posters depicting the play, to models of the secret annex. One boy, who did not excel in reading and writing, made an elaborate wooden model of the secret annex. It was the only piece of work that he completed all year, and I can still remember the proud look on his face when he carried it into the classroom and was swarmed by classmates who wanted a closer look. This unit, more than anything, engaged those students who had previously existed in the margins of the classroom community.

During the three years that I worked in this school district, I generally received positive feedback on my teaching. On March 2, 1987, the principal wrote in my formal evaluation, "Mr. Muchmore is pleasant and works well with students, parents, and staff. He is an extremely hardworking teacher who is committed to improving his skills. I am not alone in noticing this." I *was* strongly committed to being a good teacher and a good coach, and, as the principal and others observed, I *did* work extremely hard. Every day, after concluding my coaching responsibilities, I returned to my classroom in order to prepare for the next day's lessons, sometimes not leaving until 10:30 or 11:00 p.m.—and classes began the next morning at 7:00, which meant that I had to get up at 5:00 a.m. It was a grueling lifestyle, which was made even more difficult by the constant tension that I experienced in having to follow mandates that ran counter to my beliefs. Overall, I liked my job, but after three years of teaching in this school district I was ready for a change.

Returning to Graduate School

I resigned my teaching position in the midst of a fierce political battle being waged between the superintendent and several groups of unhappy parents. For various reasons, these parents, who represented a sizable portion of the community, were angry with the superintendent, and they had organized themselves well enough to vote down three consecutive property tax levies. At an emotional town meeting after the third no-vote, they had vowed that they would never allow another levy to pass until the school board acted on their mandate and replaced the superintendent.

The board, which strongly supported the superintendent, responded by hiring a university consultant to conduct a survey of the community in order to find out exactly why the tax levies had failed so that they could plan their strategy accordingly. Over the space of several weeks, a questionnaire was developed, a random sample of community members was drawn, and data were systematically collected and analyzed. Surprisingly, the results indicated no strong correlation between the community's dissatisfaction with the superintendent and their failure to pass the tax levies, and the school board used this data as a justification for giving the superintendent a new three-year contract with a substantial increase in pay. Outraged by this action, the parents worked harder than ever to make sure the next tax levy did not pass.

We teachers were mystified by the results of the survey. How had a supposedly "scientific" study failed so thoroughly to capture the tenor of the community that was obvious to those of us who lived and worked there? Some teachers felt that the university consultant must have been paid off by the school board to produce the findings they wanted. Others were skeptical about the appropriateness of using a survey methodology in the first place. To many, it seemed that simply spending some time in the community and informally interacting with the people—talking to them and listening to what they had to say—would have been a much more valid way to gain information.

In the meantime, because the school district was close to bankruptcy, we teachers were faced with a freeze on our salaries, and we were forced to use ten-year-old textbooks and rationed supplies in our overcrowded classrooms. Then, we were told that the only way to balance the budget was to release those teachers who did not have tenure, and the school board issued the following ultimatum to the voters: "Unless the next tax levy passes, thirty teachers will be laid off." I decided not to wait. I had always thought about going back to graduate school, and since my job was now in jeopardy, I decided that it was probably a good time to leave. So, I quit my job and enrolled at the University of Michigan, hoping to find solutions to some of the problems that had plagued me as a teacher.

PART II

RESEARCH STORIES

Upon arriving at the University of Michigan after four years of teaching in the public schools, I was unsure about the direction of my career. During my first semester as a new graduate student, I distinctly remember one of my professors asking, "So Jim, what do you want to do after you leave here?" The question caught me off-guard. After I leave here? I thought. I just got here. I can hardly see past next week, let alone years into the future. Then I think I mumbled something about wanting to keep my options open, nervously hoping that my lack of a clear goal was not too obvious.

Part of the reason for my indecision was the "culture shock" that I experienced as a new student at the University of Michigan. During my first few semesters in the School of Education, my thinking and disposition were heavily influenced by my lived experiences as a teacher in school districts where I had little or no voice or sense of agency. As a result, when I first arrived at the University of Michigan, I did not quite know how to deal with the intellectual freedom that I suddenly encountered, and I responded by withdrawing and keeping a low profile. During the ensuing semesters, however, I had several interactional moments or experiences that facilitated my growth and development as a scholar—experiences that Denzin (1989a) would call "epiphanies."

One of these epiphanies occurred during the winter of 1990 when I was enrolled in a course called "The Intellectual and Social History of Education." While researching a paper for this class, I came across several books that had a profound impact on my thinking—books such as John Holt's *How Children Learn* (1964) and *How Children Fail* (1967);

Carl Rogers' *Freedom to Learn* (1969); Edgar Friedenberg's *Vanishing Adolescent* (1964); Paul Goodman's *Compulsory Mis-education* (1964); Ivan Illich's *Deschooling Society* (1971) and *After Deschooling, What?* (1973); and A. S. Neill's *Summerhill* (1960). Although these books were all from a past generation and were no longer in the forefront of most discussions about education, they were completely new to me in the winter of 1990, and the more I read them the more I became intrigued by their ideas. They stimulated me to think about education in new ways. What is the meaning of education? What role do schools play in our society? How far can schools deviate from the "norm" and still be called schools? Do we really even need schools? In considering these kinds of questions, I became especially interested in the idea of home education, which was the focus of John Holt's work in the years preceding his death in 1985 (see, e.g., Holt, 1981).

Knowing that J. Gary Knowles, then a professor at the University of Michigan, had done research in the area of home education, I decided to introduce myself to him and see if I could become involved in his work. This initial meeting led to our completion and publication of an article on the origins and phases of the home education movement in the United States (Knowles, Marlow, & Muchmore, 1992) that Gary had begun on his own, and it evolved into a continuing collaborative relationship. In 1993, for example, I helped him to write a home education research proposal that was funded with me as his assistant. This project resulted in the publication of an article dealing with the lives of adults who had been home-educated as children (Knowles & Muchmore, 1995). At the same time, I also became involved with Gary's research on teacher development, which led to our presentation of a paper at the Annual Meeting of the American Educational Research Association (Muchmore & Knowles, 1993). In this paper, we described how the lives of a group of teachers had been changed through their participation on the steering committee of a professional development school. Both of these areas of research— home education and teacher development—involved life history research, an interpretive approach that I first learned about in Gary's two-semester course on qualitative research, which I took during the 1991-1992 academic year.[10] It took quite a while, however, before I was able to fully understand the epistemology of this "new" approach.

Throughout Part II, which is divided into two chapters, I chronicle the background and evolution of my work with Anna. In Chapter 3, I review some of the literature on teacher thinking. Characterized by an eclectic array of methodologies, divergent foci, and idiosyncratic terminologies, this literature is difficult to synthesize (e.g., Clark & Peterson, 1986; Elbaz, 1991; Fenstermacher, 1994; Kagen, 1992). In order to contextualize my research, I provide an overview of the main strands of this literature, with a particular focus on those studies that most influenced my work with Anna. Such studies include the work of researchers such as Barr and Duffy (1978), Buike and Duffy (1979), DeFord (1985), Duffy (1981), and Hoffman and Kugle (1982), all of whom utilized survey methods in studying teachers' conceptions of reading and writing. I also briefly describe my own survey study (Muchmore, 1994), since it was my personal experience with this methodology that led to my work with Anna.

In Chapter 4, I explore some the epistemological underpinnings of life history research, which I present as an alternative to survey approaches for studying teacher thinking. Specifically, I show that our lives are textual, in that we make sense of them through narrative, and that the dynamic through which we create meaning in these narratives is very similar to, if not nearly the same as, the dynamic through which we create meaning in written texts. Just as texts have multiple meanings that are negotiated through interpretive communities (Fish, 1980), so too do lives have multiple stories that are negotiated through the interactions between those who tell them and those who listen. As Denzin (1989b) states,

> A story that is told is never the same story that is heard. Each teller speaks from a biographical position that is unique and, in a sense, unsharable. Each hearer of a story hears from a similarly unsharable position. But these two versions of the story merge and run together into a collective, group version of the story that was told." (p. 72).

In describing how I came to understand this idea, I relate two particularly poignant experiences or "epiphanies" (Denzin, 1989a)—one in an art museum and the other in a troubling interaction with a former mentor. I conclude this chapter by addressing some of the common criticisms of life history research in terms of validity, reliability, and generalizability.

CHAPTER 3

TEACHERS' BELIEFS AND PRACTICES

During the past 20 years, there has been an increasing interest among educational researchers in understanding the lives of teachers (e.g., Ball & Goodson, 1985; Brunetti & McCormick, 2001; Cole & Knowles, 2001; Goodson, 1992). Important in this work is an emphasis on understanding teachers' thinking from *their* perspective—from the perspective of an *insider* looking around, and not from that of an *outsider* looking in. Such an emphasis has resulted in an increase in the use of narrative and life history approaches in studies of teacher thinking and teacher socialization (see, e.g., Carter, 1993; Casey, 1995; Clandinin & Connelly, 2000; Cole & Knowles, 2000, 2001; Goodson, 1992; Li, 2002). My study with Anna is consistent with this trend.

Why Study Teachers' Beliefs and Practices?

My motivation for collaborating with Anna is deeply rooted in my own personal experiences as a public school teacher. As a teacher, I thought of myself as a technician hired to implement the policies and curriculum that were mandated by the school board or the public law, rather than as a respected professional whose beliefs, opinions, and expertise were truly valued by my employers. Many times, for instance, I felt compelled to engage in practices such as explicit reading skills instruction or formulaic writing assignments—practices that were contrary to my beliefs about the holistic nature of reading and writing and the natural role they play in the lives of children. Like Cook-Gumperz (1986), I believed that literacy was largely a social phenomenon through which individuals came to create meaning in their lives, yet the board-mandated curriculum tended to view it as a mere act of technical competence. As a result, I was continually torn between knowing what I wanted to do in my classroom and often feeling compelled to do just the opposite—but, during that period, I possessed neither the time to reflect nor the ability to name this tension.

Instead, I simply observed my students, noted their distastes, and with a sense of frustration continued to provide them with more of the same, just as I felt I was supposed to. I knew of no other way to deal with this internal conflict. Each day, along with many of the other teachers in my school, I became more and more frustrated with my inability to match my practices to my beliefs—until gradually, I could feel my frustration being replaced by the cool indifference and heavy cynicism that I had often sensed among some of my older colleagues. I eventually began to view the contrast between my beliefs and my practices as simply "the way things were"—somewhat of a deep and dark professional secret that every teacher knew about but which no one ever talked about.

Although I do not believe that my story is atypical, it is one that seldom appears in the literature. Researchers have long suggested that teachers hold theoretical orientations to reading and writing which guide their instructional practices (e.g., DeFord, 1985; Duffy, 1981; Barr & Duffy, 1978; Duffy & Anderson, 1984; Harste & Burke, 1977; Kamil & Pearson, 1979), but I am aware of no studies that have attempted to understand this issue from a teacher's perspective. What role do teachers' personal life experiences play in their efforts to match their instructional practices to their underlying assumptions about literacy? What strategies do teachers employ? And how do these strategies change or evolve over time? Responses to these kinds of questions have the potential to build theory and provide policy-makers and administrators with valuable insights into ways of supporting teachers in their work.

Wading through the Literature on Teacher Thinking

In this chapter, I discuss some of the existing research on teacher thinking in which my study with Anna is situated. Vast and diffuse, this body of research is characterized by an eclectic array of methodologies, divergent foci, and idiosyncratic terminologies which make it very difficult to synthesize. Some researchers have used quantitative methods such as surveys or questionnaires (e.g., DeFord, 1985; Duffy & Metheny, 1979; Gove, 1983, Moilanen, 1989/1990), while others have used qualitative approaches ranging from case studies (e.g., Elbaz, 1983), to cases (e.g., Kagan & Tippins, 1992), to narratives (e.g., Nespor, & Barylske, 1991), to life histories (e.g., Goodson & Cole, 1993). Studies of teacher thinking have also spanned an incredibly broad range of foci, including teachers' beliefs about their roles (e.g., Janesick, 1978), their subject matter (e.g., Grossman, 1990), their planning (e.g., Bromme, 1982), their self-efficacy (e.g., Ponticell, 1993), their students (e.g., Medway, 1979), and classroom management (e.g. Rosoff, Woolfolk, & Hoy, 1991). Even the term "teacher thinking" has not been used consistently throughout this literature, as some researchers have chosen to call it "teacher beliefs" (Munby, 1982), while others have used terms ranging from "teacher knowledge" (Shulman, 1986), to "teacher conceptions" (Duffy, 1977), to "principles of practice" (Marland, 1977), to "personal practical knowledge" (Connelly & Clandinin, 1984), to "theoretical orientations" (Harste & Burke, 1977), to "teacher lore" (Schubert & Ayers, 1992). It is little wonder, therefore, that most scholars have tended to avoid tackling all of this research together, choosing instead to remain within their own individual niches.

In trying to make sense of such a massive and diffuse body of research, I find it useful to think of the literature in terms of several distinct strands. One of these strands encompasses the work of Shulman (1986, 1987) and his colleagues (e.g., Brickhouse & Bodner, 1992; Grant, 1991; Gudmundsdottir, 1987a, 1987b, 1987c, 1988/1989, 1990; Hall & Grant, 1991; Stodolsky & Grossman, 1995; Wilson, Shulman, & Richert, 1987), which evolved from the "Knowledge Growth in Teaching" project at Stanford University in the early 1980s. Through their research, Shulman's group attempted to understand how beginning high school teachers acquire knowledge in their disciplines and how this knowledge impacts their teaching. One outcome of this work has been the emergence of the concept of "pedagogical content knowledge." This term, as its name suggests, represents an amalgam between teachers' knowledge about their subject matter and their knowledge about teaching. According to Shulman (1986), it includes teachers' understanding of how to make a subject comprehensible to others using "the most powerful analogies, illustrations, examples, explanations, and demonstrations" (p. 9). It also includes their understanding of what makes the learning of specific topics easy or difficult, and an understanding of the knowledge and preconceptions that students of varying ages and backgrounds typically bring with them to particular learning situations.

Shulman's work has tended to focus exclusively on secondary teachers, and, as Fenstermacher (1994) suggests, it has tended to be more normative than descriptive—meaning that it is based on a conception of what teachers should know and be able to do in order to be successful, rather than on simply describing what they already do know and can do.

In contrast to Shulman's work is Munby's strand (e.g., Munby, 1985, 1986, 1987a, 1987b, 1987c; 1990; Munby & Russell, 1989; Russell & Johnston, 1988; Russell, Munby, Spafford, & Johnson, 1988), which has focused on the metaphors that teachers use when they talk about their work. Munby grounds his approach in the work of Lakoff and Johnson (1980), who maintain that human thought is largely metaphorical. For example, "we talk of arguments as structures that stand or collapse, of mind as if it were a container, and so forth" (Munby, 1987a, p. 379). Continuing, Munby states:

> One can assume that the speech used by teachers, or by other professionals when they talk about their work, represents something to them. If the speech is metaphorical, then it is reasonable to believe that the metaphors used reflect something of how the speaker sees or constructs professional reality (p. 380).

In order to put this assumption into practice—to understand the ways in which teachers think about curriculum—Munby conducted a series of interviews with teachers and asked them a variety of questions about their work (Munby, 1985, 1986, 1987a, 1987b, 1987c, 1990). According to Munby, the actual questions were unimportant, as the goal was simply to elicit their talk which was audiotaped and transcribed. Later, with computer assistance, these transcripts were systematically analyzed for metaphorical expressions. For example, one teacher talked of "*covering* content" (Munby, 1987b), while another mentioned "keeping the class *under* control" (Munby, 1987c). Munby maintained that these kinds of metaphors were more than just habitualized patterns of speech, arguing that they instead provided subtle insights into the ways in which these teachers thought about their work—especially when they were found to be used consistently by the same person over several interviews.

Also focusing on metaphors, but using a much less empirical-ana-lytical approach, is the work of Cole (e.g., 1988, 1989, 1990a, 1990b), which focused on teachers' implicit theories, attitudes, and beliefs about teaching. Instead of using transcripts as the data source out of which to extract metaphors as they occur in natural speech, Cole used the concept of metaphors as a tool for facilitating teachers' professional growth and development. In her conversations with teachers, she explicitly encour-aged them to express their thinking in terms of metaphors, which they could then reflect upon as they developed and refined their personal theo-ries of teaching. For example, in articulating her conception of teaching, one beginning teacher stated:

> I am reminded of the English romanticist Shelley who lik-ened the mind in creation to a fading coal that is enlivened and returned to its "transitory brilliance" by an "inconstant wind." As a teacher, I am the leader and source of inspiration in the classroom. I am the wind that propels the windmill. The students are the burning coals that brighten with inspira-tion as the wind hits them. Their intelligence is aroused when the inspiration moves them... (Cole, 1990a, p. 216).

In another study, an experienced teacher described his classroom as be-ing like a restaurant:

> I am a waiter in a comfortable restaurant. Prior to opening for the day I make arrangements which contribute to the gen-eral ambiance. Perhaps my duties go beyond that of a waiter. Perhaps I am the maitre d'. My students are the patrons and I am there to serve them, to make their visit a pleasant and worthwhile experience. I go from table to table to ensure that they are comfortable. I make suggestions from the menu and give assistance where needed.... I am kept busy but I enjoy my work because I am being of service to others (Cole, 1988, p. 13).

According to Cole, these kinds of extended metaphors serve not only as windows into the teachers' thinking, but also as a way for teachers to become more reflective about their beliefs and practices.

Another strand of research on teacher thinking is "The Teacher Lore Project" of Schubert and Ayers (1992), which began much more organically than the highly rational and systematic work of both Shulman and Munby. It started in 1985 when a group of doctoral students at the University of Illinois at Chicago—all experienced teachers and principals—asked their professor, William Schubert, to organize a study group devoted to progressive educational philosophy and practice (Ayers & Schubert, 1994). In the course of their discussions, the participants became interested in the stark contrast between the power of experiential knowledge in their daily lives and the relative absence of this knowledge in research on teaching. "Where are the voices of teachers?" they asked. "What knowledge and experiences do teachers consider most worthwhile? Why do great classroom teachers typically retire into obscurity, without being asked what they learned? What wisdom is being missed, what lessons lost?" (Ayers & Schubert, 1994, p. 107). To answer these questions, the group decided to seek out and interview teachers who were considered to be "outstanding" by their colleagues, students, or supervisors. Their goal was to create an informal archive that would chronicle these teachers' accumulated insights, ideas, beliefs, feelings, knowledge, and wisdom about teaching—in other words, their lore.

This archive has been built upon and expanded by the original participants in the study group, as well as by subsequent doctoral students and other researchers, with each adding his or her own reflections, interpretations, or further interviews. The book *Teacher Lore: Learning from our own experience* (Schubert & Ayers, 1992) represents a compilation of some of this research—with chapters ranging from Miller's (1992) autobiographical account of her own evolution as a teacher and a researcher, to Millie's (1992) study of the connections between one teacher's personal life and professional practice, to Melnick's (1992) inquiry into other teachers' knowledge of their students' out-of-school lives.

Somewhat related to the "teacher lore" strand, but arising independently, is the work of Clandinin and Connelly (1986, 1987), Connelly & Clandinin (1988, 1990) and their colleagues. Like Schubert and Ayers (1992), these scholars maintain that teachers possess a wide range of knowledge and beliefs derived from their experiences which they express in the form of stories. However, they use a different terminology. Elbaz (1983) calls it "practical knowledge," while Clandinin (1992) emphasizes its personal and idiosyncratic nature with the term "personal practical knowledge." According to Clandinin,

> [Personal practical knowledge] is knowledge that reflects the
> individual's prior knowledge and acknowledges the contex-
> tual nature of that teacher's knowledge. It is a kind of knowl-
> edge carved out of, and shaped by, situations; knowledge that
> is constructed and reconstructed as we live out our stories
> and retell and relive them through processes of reflection (p.
> 125).

This strand of research includes many studies on teacher thinking
that have utilized case study and narrative approaches. For example, Elbaz
(1983) conducted a case study of a high school English teacher, analyzing the nature of her practical knowledge and showing how it influenced
her instructional practices, while Craig (1992/1993) studied two beginning elementary teachers and explored the ways in which their personal
practical knowledge was shaped by their school contexts. Other studies
in this strand of research include works ranging from Clark's (1992/1993)
elicitation of two teachers' personal practical knowledge as a way to foster professional development, to Stratton Lemieux's (1995/1996) investi-
gation into the moral dimensions of nine teachers' personal practical
knowledge, to Olson's (1993/1995) study of the ways in which two
preservice teachers' knowledge of good teaching was formed and reformed
by both their university and student teaching experiences.

One thing that many of the studies in all of these strands have in
common is an ethic of caring and sensitivity toward teachers. Some researchers—particularly in the "teacher lore" and "personal practical"
strands—feel that teachers have too long been considered mere "subjects"
in educational research, with their experiential knowledge and beliefs
routinely discounted. They view their research as an important means for
teacher empowerment. According to Ayers (1992b), "teacher lore can be
an antidote to arid research, to prescriptive policy, to empty promises. It
can be a force for combating the culture of cynicism—that pervasive sense
of powerlessness and meaninglessness flourishing in so many schools"
(p. 158).

Since my study embodies this same ideal, and somewhat resembles
the "teacher lore" and "personal practical" strands in other ways too, one
might conclude that my work with Anna was heavily influenced by this
research. In fact, this was not the case—at least not in the beginning.
While I do value these two strands and respect the researchers who produced them, they did not play any role at all in my initial conceptualization

of the study. Instead, my research emerged independently in direct response to a completely different strand of research on teacher thinking—one which utilized surveys and questionnaires and which focused specifically upon teachers' beliefs about reading. It was my dissatisfaction with this methodology, which I experienced when conducting my own survey study of teacher thinking (Muchmore, 1994), that initially motivated my work with Anna. In the remainder of this chapter, I outline this "survey" strand of research and briefly describe the survey study that I conducted in Kentucky.

The Reading/Literacy Strand of Research on Teacher Thinking

In the area of literacy research, there is a sizable body of literature based on the notion that teachers possess identifiable theoretical orientations that guide their instructional practices (see, e.g., Clark & Peterson, 1986; DeFord, 1985; Harste & Burke, 1977; Kamil & Pearson, 1979). For example, Harste and Burke (1977) state that "both students and teachers exhibit behavior which is sufficiently systematic to allow inferences about a theory which must underlie that behavior" (p. 32), while Kamil and Pearson (1979) maintain that beliefs or models of reading and literacy "are a vital part of the instructional process, even when teachers are not consciously aware of a model's presence" (p. 10).

This strand of research can be divided into two broad categories, based largely upon their findings. While some studies have shown that there is a simple and direct connection between teachers' beliefs and practices, others have concluded that the relationship is relatively weak and quite complex. In the former category, Rupley and Logan (1986) found that teachers' beliefs about reading and literacy were consistent with their decisions about the importance of specific literacy outcomes. In their study, teachers completed a questionnaire designed to measure their literacy beliefs and then rated a list of behavioral objectives in order to indicate the practices to which they were most inclined. The results showed that beliefs which were student-centered were significantly and positively correlated with student-centered behavioral objectives. Kinzer and Carrick (1986) described a similar relationship between teachers' beliefs about how literacy develops (e.g., specific skills, whole language, or integrated) and their practices as reflected by sample lessons. They reported that when teachers were asked to select literacy lesson plans representing various orientations, they tended to choose those that were consistent with their beliefs about how literacy develops—especially for higher level areas such as comprehension and vocabulary. In another study in this category, Richardson, Anders, Tidwell, and Lloyd (1991) utilized ethnographic belief interviews to predict specific teaching practices, concluding that there was a strong relationship between teachers' beliefs about literacy and their instructional practices. Similarly, Johnson (1992) noted that English-as-a-second-language teachers who had strong beliefs about second-language instruction provided instruction that was consistent with their beliefs.

Among studies in the second category (i.e., those which concluded that the relationship between teachers' beliefs and practices was relatively weak), Hoffman and Kugle (1982) concluded that literacy "beliefs are situational and relate in complex ways to the context of instruction" (p. 6). This finding is supported by the work of Buike and Duffy (1979), Duffy (1981), Barr and Duffy (1978), and Duffy and Anderson (1984), all of whom were affiliated with Michigan State University's Institute for Research on Teaching. These researchers concluded that teachers typically hold not just one, but several conceptions of literacy, and that these conceptions are held in conjunction with a host of nonliteracy conceptions—including ideas about "classroom management, expectations of pupils, attitudes toward children, the role of feedback, the nature of child growth and development, preferences for reinforcement procedures, attitudes towards behavior problems, and others" (Buike & Duffy, 1979, p. 6). In addition, they proposed that all of these conceptions—both literacy and nonliteracy—were context-dependent, meaning that they might change according to factors such as grade level and the abilities of the readers. According to these researchers, in order for teachers' beliefs about literacy to be realized in their instructional practices, they must first be filtered through a complex web of nonliteracy conceptions and external contexts which may be overriding influences. Consequently, they claimed, the relationship between beliefs and practices is a very diluted one, if it exists at all.

One possible explanation for the divergent findings in these studies is the variety of ways in which researchers have chosen to operationally define and measure teachers' beliefs. Eisenhart, Shrum, Harding, and

Cuthbert (1988) have noted that no single definition of "beliefs" is widely accepted by the educational research community, and researchers have tended to use the term very narrowly, often couching it in their own specialized terminology. For example, Harste and Burke (1977) defined teachers' beliefs as a kind of theory or "system of assumptions through which experiences are organized and acted upon" (p. 32), and they labeled these beliefs on a continuum ranging from "skills" to "whole language."

Utilizing Harste and Burke's definition, both DeFord (1985) and Duffy and Metheny (1979) designed instruments to measure teachers' beliefs about literacy. However, they chose different ways to operationalize this definition. DeFord's (1985) instrument, which is called the "Theoretical Orientation to Reading Profile" (TORP), consists of twenty-eight statements to which teachers are required to indicate the extent of their agreement or disagreement, and it situates their beliefs on an instructional continuum ranging from phonics, to skills, to whole language. In contrast, Duffy and Metheny's (1979) "Propositions About Reading Instruction Inventory" is an instrument that defines teachers' beliefs in terms of common instructional models (i.e., basal textbooks, linear skills, interest-based, natural language, and integrated curriculum). Although both instruments seem to acknowledge that teachers' beliefs about reading can range from skills-based to holistic, they do not necessarily measure the same construct. DeFord's (1985) three-point continuum is drawn from an inspection of common teaching materials, while Duffy and Metheny's (1979) five categories are based on a review of college textbooks used in reading methods courses. Hence, while DeFord's operational definition is connected to inservice teacher practices, Duffy and Metheny's is tied to preservice teacher education.

Varying definitions can also be found in studies that have used other methods to determine teachers' beliefs—methods such as interviews (Gove, 1983; Richardson, Anders, Tidwell, & Lloyd, 1991) and ordered trees (Weidler, 1989). Gove (1983) created a structured interview protocol called the "Conceptual Framework of Reading Interview" which was based on information processing models of reading. In the interview, teachers are required to respond to a pre-set series of questions which identify their beliefs as bottom-up (e.g., Gough, 1976), top-down (e.g., Goodman, 1976) or interactive (e.g., Rumelhart, 1975/1976). In another interview study, Richardson, Anders, Tidwell, and Lloyd (1991) utilized a semi-structured interview format to elicit teachers' opinions about reading, and based on the range of teachers' responses, they constructed a continuum ranging from skills to literature. In this way, an operational definition of literacy beliefs was derived inductively from the results of the interview itself instead of being embedded in the interview a priori. Weidler (1989) selected yet another method of measuring teachers' literacy beliefs by using ordered trees, a procedure in which teachers drew diagrams to display the concepts included in their knowledge structures and how these concepts were related.

In summary, these varying methods for ascertaining teachers' literacy beliefs have involved such a diverse set of operational definitions that even though researchers may have used the same broad term of "beliefs" to describe their work, they do not necessarily refer to the same construct.

Another possible explanation for the mixed findings in these studies is the variety of ways in which teachers' practices have been ascertained. For example, while Buike and Duffy (1979) used direct observations and audiotapes in order to document teachers' classroom practices, Kinzer and Carrick (1986) used a proxy for direct observations by presenting teachers with a series of lesson plans that reflected various theoretical orientations and requiring them to select the one they would be most likely to use under ideal classroom conditions. The use of such differing methods may, in part, explain why the results of these two studies were different. It may be that there is a closer relationship between teachers' beliefs and practices when this relationship is not mediated by the external contexts of teaching. After all, as I discovered through my own experiences as a teacher, classroom conditions are seldom "ideal."

A final possible explanation for the mixed findings in this strand of research is that most of the studies have focused on relatively small numbers of teachers—usually between 20 and 40 (c.f., Buike & Duffy, 1979; Johnson, 1992; Hoffman & Kugle, 1982; Kinzer & Carrick, 1986). Since Duffy and Metheny (1979) noted that some teachers seemed to have mixed or confused beliefs that were not consistent with any single theoretical orientation to literacy, it is possible that in studies with such small numbers of teachers, the overall relationship between beliefs and practices may have been confounded by the presence of a few teachers who did not have dominant beliefs.

Conducting My Own Survey of
Teachers' Beliefs and Practices

As a new graduate student at the University of Michigan, I initially encountered the survey strand of research on teacher thinking in the context of a course on "reading disability." Having personally experienced the challenge of trying to match my pedagogical practices to my underlying beliefs about reading and writing, I hoped these studies might help me to better understand some of the problems that I had faced as a teacher. It did not matter that their style, their tone, and their findings were geared much more toward educational researchers than toward classroom teachers. This kind of research—which was based upon traditional notions of scientific inquiry—was what I had read as an undergraduate, and it was the only kind of research that I knew about or valued at the time.

In December, 1990, after completing my third semester as a doctoral student, I took a brief leave from my graduate studies at the University of Michigan and worked for six months as a Chapter 1 Reading Consultant for the Kentucky Department of Education.[11] I had personal reasons for wanting to return to my home state at this time, but I was also intrigued by the flurry of national attention that Kentucky's schools were receiving after the passage of the House Bill 940 in 1989. Widely described as "the most comprehensive, innovative reform legislation ever passed by any state in recent history" (Steffy, 1993, p. xiii), this far-reaching law mandated a series of radical changes in the state's public schooling system—including the implementation of performance-based assessment; the establishment of site-based management; and the abolishment of kindergarten, first, second, and third grades in favor of a multi-age classrooms. Wanting to be involved in this massive reform effort in some small way, I sought and obtained a position as a Chapter 1 Reading Consultant, a job which I held until the Department of Education was abolished and reformed in July, 1991.

During the time that I worked in Kentucky, I conducted a study of teachers' beliefs and practices similar to those that I described earlier. As part of my job, I designed and administered a survey of the beliefs and practices of all the state's Chapter 1 reading teachers. This population included more than 1200 teachers, which, to the best of my knowledge, was by far the largest number of teachers ever to have participated in a survey study of literacy beliefs and practices.

My survey had three main sections: beliefs, practices, and demographics. The beliefs section was similar to the instruments created by DeFord (1985) and Duffy and Metheny (1979). It consisted of twelve propositional statements to which the teachers responded on a five-point scale, ranging from "strongly agree" to "strongly disagree." These propositional statements were consistent with four theoretical orientations to reading problems, which I based upon the work of Wixson and Lipson (1991). Each of the four theoretical orientations was represented by three items which I then averaged in order to produce composite belief scores.

The section of the survey dealing with the teachers' practices consisted of four instructional vignettes that described plausible classroom scenarios, and the teachers again used a five-point scale to indicate the extent to which these scenarios matched what they felt they did in their classrooms. Each vignette was consistent with one of the four theoretical orientations to reading problems.

The demographics section dealt with the teachers' backgrounds and professional activities—including years of experiences, number of years since their last college course in reading methods, their professional memberships, and the journals they read on a regular basis.

To determine the overall relationship between the teachers' beliefs and practices, I constructed a contingency table, performed a Chi-Square test, and calculated Cramer's *V*. Then, to determine which cells of the contingency table were responsible for the relationship, I analyzed the standardized residuals of the observed and expected frequencies in the manner described by Everitt (1977). Finally, I compared the professional characteristics among those teachers who had beliefs and practices that were consistent with the same perspective.

The results indicated that most of the teachers surveyed did not have matching beliefs and practices. However, those whose beliefs and practices did match were more professionally involved. They had more recently taken a college course in reading, were more active in their reading of journals, and were frequent participants in professional organizations.

A more detailed account of the methods, results, and implications of this study can be found in an article published in *Remedial and Special Education* (Muchmore, 1994).

CHAPTER 4

UNDERSTANDING LIFE HISTORY RESEARCH

I felt proud when I completed my survey of Kentucky's Chapter 1 reading teachers. It was a massive undertaking which I accomplished entirely on my own. From mailing and collecting the surveys, to entering the data on the computer, to calculating the statistics, to writing the findings, I did everything by myself. In fact, I came to view this study as kind of a personal work of art—my creation, my achievement. It was the same kind of satisfaction that I got when I was running track and had completed a particularly challenging workout. At the same time, however, I had a nagging feeling that my accomplishment may not have been entirely worthwhile. Even before I began to analyze the data, I had doubts about using a methodology that treated teachers as "subjects" and reduced their thinking to items on a survey.

In order to ameliorate this concern—even if only partially—I tried to be as respectful as possible toward the teachers in my writing (see Muchmore, 1994). For example, I was careful not to use language that might be construed as condescending, and I consciously avoided framing my recommendations in terms of mandates. In fact, when I submitted my article for publication, one of the reviewers wrote, "The discussion should include mention of the need to provide district-sponsored and mandatory staff development," to which I steadfastly responded:

> I am not comfortable in advocating the need for administrators to provide *mandatory* staff development for teachers. Such a recommendation conflicts with my personal stance toward teachers' professional development in which I ques-

tion the effectiveness of top-down mandates in changing
teachers' thinking. I am much more comfortable in simply
advocating the establishment of conditions that would be
conducive toward teachers' professional development without making their participation mandatory.

Over time, I became increasingly aware that there was something funda-
mentally wrong with a research methodology that transformed teachers'
beliefs and practices into a collection of numbers and analyzed them using statistics. What had happened to all of the teachers? What had happened to their voices? To their experiences? With a few strokes on my
computer keyboard, I had reduced their lives to a contingency table.

I also had reservations about my writing style, which, although technically competent, displayed the same detached, third-person voice that I
had learned as an undergraduate. This style of writing seemed to lend a
false air of authority to my study—an air of precision and certainty. By
the time the article was published, I had long since left my job in Kentucky, and, following the reorganization of the Department of Education,
most of my colleagues had left as well. Nevertheless, I did send a copy to
a former colleague, who was then working at a school district in Kentucky, and I told him of my ambivalence. His reply was upbeat and encouraging:

> To say that I was impressed with your article would be an
> understatement. As someone who dabbles at writing, I'm al-
> ways impressed when someone I know puts together a uni-
> fied sequence of words in a concise, coherent manner. I rarely
> read anything in print where I can't find at least one poor
> choice of words or one word too many. Here—nothing!...
> Sure, it was a little dry, but the audience isn't reading this
> journal for entertainment. They read it for what you have given
> them—a specific slant on an instructional topic supported by
> evidence.

In spite of these kind words of support, however, I still felt uncomfortable about what I had done. The entire structure of my study seemed
far too rigid. It forced teachers into my pre-existing conceptual scheme,
which, although carefully conceived, may not have represented their actual thinking. The process was somewhat like pouring liquid plaster into
a mold, allowing it to harden, removing the mold, and then announcing,

"I have discovered the shape of plaster!" My survey was a mold that had twisted and contorted the teachers' thinking into ready-made categories. Perhaps nowhere was this metaphor more applicable than in the remarks that some of the teachers had written in the margins of their returned surveys. As I was entering the data on my computer, I was surprised by how often I encountered notations such as "yes, but..." or "sometimes, but not always" as some teachers obviously struggled to make *my* conceptual scheme fit *their* thinking. Of course, my statistical data analysis approach provided no way to account for these comments, so I simply ignored them. Also, in the back of my mind, I could not help but remember the voter survey commissioned by my former school district and the wide discrepancy between its findings and the perspectives of those of us who lived and worked in the community. In short, I questioned its validity.

Even if my survey were accepted as a valid way to understand teachers' thinking, it still had a serious limitation. Although I was able to determine general trends for a large number of teachers, I learned nothing about the specific nature of the relationship between their beliefs and practices and how they experienced this relationship on an individual level.

The more I thought about it, the more I realized that my interest in this topic was not a detached academic one, as the language in my article suggested. Instead, it was very personal. Administering surveys, fiddling with variables, and performing statistics—while satisfying as an intellectual exercise—had done little to help me in understanding the problems that had troubled me as a teacher. I needed a different methodology—a different approach—and, strongly influenced by my ongoing work with Gary Knowles, I gradually moved toward a life history approach.

What is Life History Research?

Although it can be traced to the informal life stories of Native Americans in the nineteenth century (Polkinghorne, 1988) and to later more sophisticated works such as Thomas and Znaniecki's *The Polish Peasant in Europe and America* (1927) and Shaw's *The Jack-Roller* (1930), life history research has never been widely accepted by mainstream researchers in the social sciences (e.g., Becker, 1978; Bertaux, 1983; Faraday & Plummer, 1979; Fischer, 1983). Typically plagued by apparent "problems" with validity, reliability, and generalizability, it has long existed on the fringes of methodological acceptability—often being relegated to the role of simply providing a bit of color in studies based on "more rigorous" methodologies. During the past fifteen years, however, researchers such as Denzin (1989a), Donmoyer (1990), Eisner (1991), Guba and Lincoln (1989), and Kirk and Miller (1986), have begun to question the appropriateness of using concepts such as validity, reliability, and generalizability as criteria for evaluating qualitative inquiry. As a result, life history research has recently experienced somewhat of a resurgence, especially in the field of education[12] (see, e.g., Casey, 1993; Cohen, 1991; Cole, 1994; Cole & Knowles, 2001; Goodson, 1992).

Epistemologically, life history research has a basis in the sociological tradition of symbolic interactionism in which meaning is viewed as a social creation achieved through human interactions that are mediated by language or symbols. According to Blumer (1969), this concept rests on three basic premises:

> The first premise is that human beings act toward things on the basis of the meanings that the things have for them.... The second premise is that the meaning of such things is derived from, or arises out of, the social interaction that one has with one's fellows. The third premise is that these meanings are handled in, and modified through an interpretative process used by the person in dealing with the things he encounters (p. 2).

In essence, doing life history research is an interpretive endeavor, much like reading a text.

The metaphor of a life as a text is rooted in the work of anthropologists such as Winner (1978), Geertz (1983), Bruner (1986), Boon (1986), and Brown (1987), who argue that human experiences can only be expressed and understood through symbolic statements which are in essence social texts. Whether oral or written, these "texts" are fictional narrative productions that enable individuals to make sense of their lives and to share this sense with others. For example, when I related my personal story as a beginning teacher in Part I of this book, I transformed my lived experience into a work of fiction. It was fiction because no matter how completely I told it and no matter how closely you (the reader) read it, you could never experience it in the same way that I did—nor, for that matter, would I ever be able to re-experience it in exactly the same way that I did when it originally occurred. Instead, acting together, we jointly constructed a unique fictional version of my lived experience.

When lives are viewed as texts, it becomes inappropriate to evaluate the efficacy of the life history approach by the standards of objectivity, validity, reliability, and generalizability—which are the hallmarks of science. Instead, it is more appropriate to evaluate the goodness of this research by some of the same standards that are used in reader response literary criticism. For example, literary critics such as Iser (1978), Tompkins (1980), and Fish (1980) argue against the notion of objective interpretations, proposing instead that a text cannot be understood apart from the effect that it has on a reader. The text, they argue, does not determine interpretation; rather the interpretation determines the text. Holland (1980) states,

> ...all of us, as we read, use the literary work to symbolize and finally to replicate ourselves. We work out through the text our own characteristic patterns of desire and adaptation. We interact with the work, making it part of our own psychic economy and making ourselves part of the literary work—as we interpret it. For, always, this principle prevails: identity re-creates itself (p. 24).

When applied to life history research, Holland's idea suggests that researchers do not simply compile someone's life history as if it were an objective entity existing outside the interactions in which it is elicited. Instead, it is always jointly constructed by the participant and the researcher (see Gudmundsdottir, 1992). Because the only way that a researcher can make sense of someone's life is through the lenses of his or her own experiences, the resulting life history is always as much the researcher's story as it is the participant's. This is why this book, which began as a study of Anna, ultimately became a study of myself as well. All research is inherently autobiographical.

Nevertheless, this concept seemed intuitively wrong to me when I first encountered it—so deeply was my thinking rooted in the values and epistemology of science. What exactly does it mean to be a joint constructor of a life story? Telling one's story is like filling a container with water, I thought. You pour it out; it lands in the container; and there it stands, ready to be analyzed. While I liked the idea of doing life history research because it resonated with my childhood memories of listening to my grandmother's stories, I had serious misgivings about using an approach that seemed so "soft" and "unscientific." It was not until I had two particularly poignant experiences or epiphanies (Denzin, 1989a)—one in an art museum and the other in a troubling conversation with a former mentor—that I gradually began to shed my discomfort.

A Life History as an Artistic Interpretation

My first epiphany occurred in the unlikely setting of an art gallery. While attending a conference at Wayne State University in Detroit in April, 1992, I casually wandered into an area where some graduate students in the Fine Arts Program were displaying their work. It was a small room, close to the site of the conference, and a friend and I entered simply to pass the time while awaiting the start of the next session. The walls were covered with paintings—some of them abstract and others more traditional—and several sculptures rested upon pedestals that were scattered throughout the room. It all seemed very ordinary. We hastily glanced at a few of the pieces and were about to leave when I suddenly noticed an unusual object mounted on the back wall. It was a wooden box, about the size of a medicine cabinet, and it contained two large porcelain doors. Conspicuously hand-molded before they had been fired and hardened, these porcelain doors contained an unusual series of symmetrical cells, much like a honeycomb, which gave the entire object a strangely organic quality. It was almost as if the box had sprouted from the wall naturally, rather than having been placed there by human hands.

Moving closer, I studied its appearance and wondered exactly what it was supposed to be. Old and weathered, the wood invited my touch— yet I was reluctant to do so. Art is for viewing, I thought, not for touching. I paused for a moment and nervously glanced over my shoulder. Was anyone looking? No. I quickly reached out and moved my fingers along the wooden surface. Nothing happened. No alarms sounded and no one shouted at me to stop, so I ventured further and peered behind one of the porcelain doors.

It did not take much effort for me to open the door; it was perfectly balanced on two small hinges. Someone had obviously constructed it with a great deal of skill. As the heavy porcelain door slowly swung open, I was startled to see a face staring back out at me. It was a photograph of a young man. It looked like a high school yearbook picture, only it had been blown up to a much larger size and embossed on a thin, irregular layer of porcelain. I opened the other door to get a better look. The photograph was old, probably from the late 1960s or early 1970s, but the student's expression was timeless. With long dark hair and the faint beginnings of a mustache, he struck a defiant pose. It was a familiar look—a look of student resistance—which I knew well from my own days as a public school teacher. He's a "burnout," I thought, as I quickly assigned a meaning to the photograph. Moving closer, I noticed a small crack in the porcelain emanating from one of the student's eyes and gradually thickening as it spread across his face to the edge of the porcelain—a pristine photograph, marred by a jagged crack. Yes, I thought, this student must be the archetype of a high school "burnout." That must be what the artist is trying to depict. I thought I had figured it out.

While I stood there examining the photograph, I suddenly noticed two other doors beneath the porcelain ones—these made of glass—and through them I could see what looked like six small drawers. I wondered what might be inside them. I wanted to look, but felt uncomfortable. But, the artist must have intended for viewers to interact with his work, I reasoned. Otherwise, he would not have placed it in such a public location.

Once again, I nervously glanced around before hastily opening the two glass doors and pulling out one of the drawers. My heart beat faster as I looked inside. I fully expected someone to yell at me, "Hey, don't touch that!" But, again, no warning came. Inside the drawer, I found a couple of small, laminated cards. The first one said:

> *Student Identification Card*
> *Highland Park High School, 1968-69*
> *Steve Lenzo, Age 15, Grade 10*

There was a photograph on this card, which I immediately recognized as the same boy whose picture was embossed on the porcelain. I picked up the card and held it in my hand. Suddenly, this boy was no longer an anonymous "burn-out." He actually had a name.

The other card was much newer. It showed a grown man with short-cropped hair, a beard, and glasses. He hardly resembled the boy in the first picture, but the name was the same. "Steven Lenzo," it said, "South Bronx High School."

So the boy must have become a teacher, I thought, realizing that my initial interpretation may have been wrong. After all, burnouts did not become teachers, did they? I now had two pieces of information, and the young man's life began to take on a new meaning.

In search of additional clues, I reached deeper into the same drawer and found a tattered old report card. It listed the following grades:

Advanced Biology	*A*
Geometry I	*A*
Spanish I	*A*
Physical Education	*A*
World Culture	*A*
Speech	*B*

All *A*s and one *B*. These were definitely not the grades of a burnout. I wondered how my initial impression could have been so wrong.

By now, since no one had challenged me, I became less concerned about interacting with this work of art, and simply wanted to know more about the man, Steven Lenzo. Who was he? Who was the artist? What was the purpose of this box? What was inside the rest of the drawers? I imagined the possibilities—just as if I were back at my grandmother's house looking through her old trinket box. Inside another drawer, I found a silver whistle on an old frayed lanyard, similar to the one that I still have from my former days as a high school track coach. Perhaps he was a coach too, I thought. In posing this question, I suddenly became aware of how subjective my interpretations had been up to this point. Instead of *uncovering* Steve Lenzo's life, or "pouring it into a container," I realized that I was actually *creating* a version of his life—one that was inextricably linked to my own, for it was through the lens of my own life experiences that I was making sense of these objects.

Beneath the whistle, there was an envelope that contained a note. Pausing before opening it, I once again began to feel uneasy—almost as if I had broken into someone's house and was rummaging through his private possessions. I felt like an intruder. First, I had opened the porcelain doors. Then, I had opened the glass doors and pulled out a drawer. Now, I was about to breach yet another barrier by opening this envelope. I wondered if I had gone too far. After all, who was I to poke around this man's life? But then I remembered where I was. I was in an art gallery—a public place—and this wooden box was being displayed as a work of art. Nevertheless, I was still nervous as I opened the envelope and pulled out a slip of paper. It was a memo typed on a half-sheet of stationary from

Highland Park High School. Frail and yellow with age, it said:

> To: *Steve Lenzo*
> *From: All the students of HPHS*
> *Subject: Long Hair*
>
> *Since school opened, we have tolerated your long hair without complaining, but you have let it go too far. We hereby officially ask you to get a haircut. If it is not cut within ten days, we will have to cut it ourselves.*
> *FAIR WARNING*
>
> *Sincerely,*
> *Highland Park High School*

Surely this must have been a joke, I thought. Perhaps he was a burnout after all. Or was he? I read it again more carefully. *From: All the students of HPHS...* Yes, it must have been a joke. Otherwise, it would have been signed by a single person—the principal perhaps—not the high school at large. Steve Lenzo must have had a good sense of humor, or at least his classmates did. I carefully refolded the slip of paper, inserted it back into the envelope, and returned it to the drawer, just as I had found it.

Opening the next drawer, I found five photographs. The first was of a smiling adolescent who looked like the boy in the initial yearbook picture embossed on porcelain, only he was younger and his hair was much shorter. I turned it over and read the back: "1964 World's Fair." The second picture revealed a much older version of the same boy, now grown and holding a baby. Could this be Steve's child? Next, there was a black and white photograph of him standing next to a young woman. Perhaps this was his wife, or at least the mother of the child. I hoped the two remaining pictures would provide some definitive answers. One showed a different man—definitely not Steve—holding a different baby. Who was this man? A friend? A brother? I did not know. The final picture revealed a wrecked car—horribly twisted, almost beyond recognition. Perhaps Steve had been killed in this car. Maybe this whole work of art was intended to serve as a memorial to him. I did not know.

Opening another drawer, I found a whole new set of artifacts that further confounded my ongoing interpretations. There was a Washtenaw County Sheriff's Department patch, along with a passport and some foreign money. What did this mean? Had Steve been a law enforcement officer? Had he traveled overseas? Then, I saw a letter written in Spanish and a leather necklace laced with a large blue stone. What did it mean? The drawers were like a row of windows to a large room, and each time I peered into a different window, the view was slightly different.

Coming to the last two drawers, I hoped that I would finally be able to make sense of everything—but instead I encountered only a few more scattered pieces of this man's life. There was a crumpled draft card, a collection of seeds, and a pocket-sized "Smoky-the-Bear" calendar book for the current year. No answers here, just more questions. Had he avoided the draft? Perhaps he had traveled to Mexico during the Vietnam War. And what about the seeds? Could they be drugs? I now envisioned Steve as a burnout again.

The last item was a stamped envelope with a very recent postmark. Inside, I found a letter that had been handwritten on a single white sheet of stationary. As I read it, the whole story once again began to take on a new meaning. It said:

Dear Peter,

> *Sorry it has taken me so long to package this. We just got back from a four day trip to Portland, combined business and pleasure trip. Joe B. was great even during the nine hour car ride. We saw lots of my old friends, their kids, and spent a couple of nights in a hotel in downtown Portland. Took Joe. B. to the zoo too, he liked the monkeys. Here's a brief explanation of the enclosed items.*

> *(1) Cards from South Bronx and Highland Park High School.*
> *(2) Canceled passport from trips to Switzerland and Central America.*
> *(3) The photo Jennifer and I used for our wedding invitation.*
> *(4) Sheriff's patch from my corrections officer uniform.*
> *(5) Draft card from 1972.*
> *(6) Resolution from Honduras Forest Service declaring the town of El Porvenir's watershed to be protected forest zone.*
> *(7) A 50 Cordoba note from Nicaragua worth about a penny in 1987.*
> *(8) Whistle I used while lifeguarding at Savyatich, 1972.*

(9) Jade necklace of carved foot supposed a Mayan relic given
me by an anthropology student in Guatemala.
(10) A coin from Peru (1/2 sol).
(11) Some grass seeds known as "lagrima de san Pedro" in
Honduras and worn around baby's necks to ward off
evil spirits.
(12) The Smoky calendar is for you.

Love,
Steve

After the conference at Wayne State had ended, I went home to Ann Arbor but could not stop thinking about my experience with this work of art. I wanted to know more about Steven Lenzo and the artist, Peter, who had chronicled his life. Early the next morning, I drove back to Detroit and returned to the gallery. When I got there, however, I was surprised to find that the work of art was gone. In fact, the entire room was empty; nothing remained. It was almost as if I had dreamed the whole thing. Going into a nearby office, I saw a secretary and asked what had happened to the exhibit. Before she could reply, I imagined her saying, "I don't know what you're talking about. There hasn't been an art exhibit in this building for years." In reality, however, she offered a more plausible explanation. The exhibit was over, and all of the artists had removed their work earlier that morning.

"Was a guy named Peter here?" I asked.

"You must mean Peter Lenzo," she said. "Yes, he was here. In fact, I think he's still in the building.

"What does he look like?"

"He's a tall man in his late thirties with long dark hair pulled back into ponytail. You can't miss him."

Armed with this information, I raced back out into a hall and immediately spotted a man walking toward me who fit the description.

"Are you Peter Lenzo?" I shouted.

"Yes, I am," he replied with an inquisitive look on his face. "What can I do for you?"

"My name is Jim Muchmore," I said. "I'm a graduate student at the University of Michigan. I saw your work yesterday, and it made a really strong an impression on me. I came back for another look...."

Peter smiled as I spoke, and we then had a long conversation about his work. He told me that he called his wooden box a "reliquary," meaning that it was a receptacle or repository for keeping or storing artifacts. He said that he had made several of these reliquaries—one for each of his siblings in order to repay them for helping to support him while he was in graduate school at Wayne State. This particular exhibit, he told me, had also served as his final project for his Master of Fine Arts Degree (Lenzo, 1992). He smiled when I told him how I had interacted with it—how I had touched it—and he seemed amused by my reaction. He explained that all of his work was intensely personal, yet he had purposely designed it to be as inviting as possible. He wanted people to struggle, as I had, with the tension between wanting to explore it and feeling that it was wrong.

After briefly chatting about his family, Peter invited me back to his studio to let me re-explore his brother's reliquary.[13] It looked different there, resting on the studio floor. It seemed smaller and much less mysterious. Yet, as soon as I opened the drawers and started examining the artifacts, I once again found myself trying to piece together Steve's life— this time with the added knowledge gained from my conversation with Peter. With each new encounter, the artifacts took on a slightly different meaning. For instance, Peter told me that Steve was once involved in a serious automobile accident. The entire car had been destroyed, yet he had miraculously survived—his only injury being a large circular bruise on his chest caused by the impact of his body against the steering wheel. I thought about this story when I saw the picture of the wrecked car again, and I remembered a similar event in my own life in which my head had shattered the windshield during a head-on auto accident when I was in college. I was fortunate to walk away from that accident completely unscathed—no cuts, no bruises, not even a bump.

In making this reliquary, Peter collaborated with his brother to create a kind of living portfolio. Just like the items in my grandmother's trinket box, each object told a different story, and as the interpreter it was my job to piece them together to form a unified whole. The soundness of my interpretations rested not on their consistency with an objective truth, but instead on their own internal consistency—the extent to which they made sense within a particular context. I came to this interpretive endeavor with a unique set of personal experiences that helped to inform my initial impressions of his brother—impressions that continually changed and re-formulated with the discovery of each new artifact—until eventually my interpretations could account for all of the information at hand. Heavily influenced by my own life history, as well as the time and context of my encounter, my interpretations were highly subjective and idiosyncratic. Another person might have seen things quite differently, or if I had encountered the work of art at a different time or in a different place, I too might have constructed a very different version of Steve's life—for as Denzin (1989b) states, "No reading or writing of a life is ever complete or final.... There can only be multiple versions of a biography or autobiography" (p. 46-47).

"That's Not Research!"

About a year-and-a-half after my encounter with Peter Lenzo's art, I had another epiphany that helped to shape my understanding of life history research; however, this one was not nearly as pleasant. It was the summer of 1993, and I had travelled to Tennessee to visit friends from college. While there, I also stopped by to see one of my old Vanderbilt professors. He was the same professor to whom I was afraid to pose the question, "Why is it important to read?", and he was the same professor who often spoke disparagingly of teachers who did not use scientifically-proven methods. Nevertheless, he had done much to help me over the years since I had graduated, and I enjoyed talking with him.

My visit began on a friendly basis. First, he told me about some of the courses he was teaching, while I told him about some of my work at the University of Michigan. But when the conversation turned toward my study of Anna, the tenor of our interaction suddenly changed.

"I'm doing a life history study of one teacher exploring her beliefs and practices," I said. "She's an excellent teacher, with twenty-five years of experience, and she has a very unique, student-centered approach. I'm really interested in finding out how she got to this point in her career...." No sooner had these words left my mouth than I saw his eyes narrow and his jaw stiffen. I could tell that he did not approve.

"That's not research," he interrupted, without allowing me to finish. He then launched into an extended oration about the perceived shortcomings of interpretive research. The vehemence of his comments caught me completely off-guard. "What good does it do to study one teacher?" he asked. "How does that contribute to the research base on teacher thinking? Everyone walking down the street has a set of beliefs that guide their actions. So what! What makes this one teacher worth studying—as opposed to any other teacher? And how can you ever make generalizations when your sample size is only one? What bothers me about this kind of 'research' is that people tend to write nothing more than compelling stories to support whatever position they already hold. I'm sorry, but that's not rigorous; that's not objective; and that's not research!"

I tried to defend my position, but he would not stop long enough for me to reply—and even if he had, I doubt that he would have listened. He appeared to be very upset—bitter even—that interpretive research had attained a stature of credibility within the field of education, and he was in no mood for a polite discussion. He had never spoken to me like this before and I was quite taken aback. Our one-sided conversation continued until I finally realized that we were not going to be able to mend our difference and part on good terms. This was the end of our relationship.

I have not revisited that professor since I left his office that day, and I probably never will. However, I still think about what he said—and I often think about how I would have responded if I could go back and relive that moment. There were two main points to his criticism. First, he seemed to feel that life history and narrative research were less rigorous than more traditional forms of educational research—that they were somehow more susceptible to the individual biases of the researcher. There was nothing to prevent a person from simply writing a piece of fiction with no basis in an actual experience and then presenting it as being true. In other words, he felt that life history research did not measure up to the validity criteria of the more traditional forms of educational research that dealt with hypothesis testing, cause-and-effect relationships, and standardized procedures.

Second, he seemed to feel that an in-depth study of one teacher was not research because it did not produce knowledge or insights that could be generalized to other teachers. The goal of educational research, he felt, is to produce a body of knowledge from which human behavior can be predicted and controlled—and a necessary component for this outcome is random sampling, which means that the subjects in a study must be indiscriminately selected from among all the individuals in a given population. And, the sample size must be large enough to subdue the impact of those subjects who may be unusual in some way or otherwise not representative of the population from which they were drawn. In essence, the goal of this kind of research is to characterize the average, not to study the unique.

If given the opportunity, I would have told my former professor that these criticisms were rooted in the epistemological assumptions of mainstream quantitative social science—not symbolic interactionism or interpretive inquiry.

It is tempting for interpretive researchers to simply dismiss concepts such as validity and generalizability as being inappropriate criteria for judging the goodness of their work (Kvale, 1989), and leave it at that. However, at the risk of resurrecting a tired and worn-out debate between quantitative and qualitative methods, I feel that my former professor raised some important questions that do need to be addressed. For example, how do interpretive researchers warrant their knowledge claims, if not by comparing them to an objective reality? If validity is an irrelevant concept, then how do we distinguish between a study that "gets it right" and one that "misses the mark?" And, what is the purpose of interpretive research if not to produce knowledge that can be generalized to other people, places, and times?

To answer these questions, I feel it is important to first understand how researchers who work with cause-and-effect relationships warrant their knowledge claims and generalize their findings. Campbell and Stanley (1966) distinguish between two kinds of validity—internal and external—which mirror the concerns voiced by my former professor. Internal validity is achieved when the results of a study can be attributed exclusively to the independent variables and not to any other variables that were not controlled, while external validity is achieved when a causal relationship between two variables can be generalized to different groups of people in different settings at different times. According to Cook and Campbell (1979), there are several specific threats to each kind of validity—including history, maturation, testing, selection, mortality, and others for internal validity, and various statistical interaction effects for external validity—and it is the responsibility of the researcher to systematically rule out each of these threats in order to ensure the validity and generalizability of his or her study.

In practice, however, Mishler (1990) points out that there is no universal procedure for ensuring the trustworthiness of any study; there is no cookbook recipe to follow. Indeed, Cook and Campbell (1979) readily admit that it is entirely the responsibility of the researcher to weigh, analyze, and evaluate the relative merits of each of these threats in making knowledge claims. In other words, it is admittedly a highly subjective process—which, unfortunately, tends to be obscured by the detached, third-person style of writing found in many research reports. My former professor might argue that this subjectivity is inconsequential—that as long as the results can be reproduced by other researchers who work independently, we can be reasonably certain that the results are valid. But, I would respond that reliability is no guarantor of validity. As Kirk and Miller (1986) observe, it is possible for researchers to be reliably wrong.

In addition, readers of traditional research reports are often provided with such scant information about the way that the study was actually conducted—receiving instead "an idealized version of *the* scientific method" (Mishler, 1990, p. 423)—that they usually have little or no basis for judging the author's knowledge claims, other than to accept his or her word that they are indeed valid. This blind faith in the integrity of the researcher, masked by an artificial aura of objectivity, can sometimes have disastrous results, such as in the case where a University of Michigan doctoral student in genetics fabricated data in a series of major leukemia studies (Wahlberg, 1996). According to his academic advisor, this student was considered to be a highly capable researcher; he had been hand-picked to work on a project sponsored by the prestigious Center for Human Genome Research of the National Institute of Health in Bethesda, Maryland. "I had no evidence, in frequent interactions with the individual over the course of three years, to question his honesty," the advisor wrote in a painful letter of apology to his colleagues. "Even in retrospect, I am not sure how these deceptions could have been uncovered sooner" (p. A8). Through this statement, the advisor was tacitly admitting that there are few safeguards for ensuring the validity of a study should a dishonest scientist decide to fabricate data—a position which challenges my former professor's contention that interpretative research is somehow more susceptible to fabrication.

In fact, life history and narrative research may actually be *more* robust than quantitative studies in terms of trustworthiness. According to Charmaz (1995), ethnographers and qualitative researchers work with data that is "self-correcting" (p. 51). "We get closer to lived experience than journalists and than most of our colleagues in the social sciences," she says. "Because our analyses *start* with our research participant's meanings, intentions and actions, we are much less likely to force our data into preconceived categories" (p. 51). In contrast, quantitative models of research require fitting the data into preconceived categories, which may distort or misrepresent the issues or questions that the research participants themselves deem most important. When researchers live and work with their subjects over an extended period of time and shape their analyses through a collaborative effort, the chance that they will "get it wrong" is greatly reduced.

Even if a life history researcher were to fabricate an account in the same way that the geneticist fabricated his data, it may still possess merit—for the more important question to ask in evaluating a story is not, "Is it true?" but instead, "What does it mean?"[14] For example, a novel which is not true in a literal sense can nevertheless have a profound meaning for those who read it. I immediately think of Jesse Stuart's *The Thread That Runs So True* (1949) and Leo Tolstoy's *Childhood, Boyhood, and Youth* (1912)—both fictional autobiographies, one of a teacher and the other of a student, which have strongly impacted my thinking about education and influenced my practice as a teacher. A fabricated life history—if plausible, well-written, and internally coherent—can still have value for those who choose to read it, while a fabricated study on the genetic origins of leukemia is completely useless.[15]

The second part of my former professor's criticism—that researchers cannot make generalizations from an in-depth study of one teacher—is based on a limited notion of generalizability. Firestone (1993) identifies three broad arguments for generalizing from data—sample-to-population extrapolation, analytic generalization, and case-to-case transfer. I feel that my former professor was relying exclusively upon the first argument while ignoring the latter two. Sample-to-population extrapolation is based upon probability theory, which assumes that the characteristics of a randomly drawn sample are statistically equivalent to the characteristics of the population from which it was drawn. This kind of generalizability is most commonly associated with opinion surveys and quasi-experimental studies.

The second argument, analytic generalization, is made when researchers attempt to generalize the findings of a particular study to a broader theory. For instance, Grossman (1990) used a case study approach to explore the theory that college graduates could become successful teachers without taking subject-specific teaching methods courses. After studying six beginning English teachers—three of whom had been through a teacher education program while the other three had not—she concluded that subject-specific pedagogical coursework made a positive difference in the ways in which these teachers approached their subject matter and taught their students, and she suggested that policy makers should think twice before waiving teacher certification requirements that include traditional university-based teacher preparation. While this kind of study, with just six participants, does not allow the author to make sample-to-population generalizations, it does "help provide the analyses necessary to build a richer conceptualization of the teacher education curriculum and its influence on how prospective teachers learn to teach" (Grossman, 1990, p. 147).

According to Firestone (1993), the third argument for generalizability, case-to-case transfer, is probably the least familiar to educational researchers. It occurs when "a person in one setting considers adopting a program or idea from another one" (Firestone, 1993, p. 17). For example, when I read Jesse Stuart's (1949) fictionalized account of his life as teacher in rural Kentucky during the 1920s, I transferred many of his ideas and experiences to my own situation as a teacher in the 1980s. Although the times and settings of our experiences were different, his writing nevertheless inspired in me a way of thinking about children and teaching that ultimately transcended these differences. In fact, as a beginning teacher, I found this kind of writing to be much more useful in helping me to deal with the everyday problems of teaching than the numerous quantitative studies on teacher effectiveness that were included in my college coursepacks.

One explanation for why this third argument for generalizability tends to be more obscure than the other two is that the responsibility for making judgments about what generalizes from setting to setting rests with the reader instead of with the writer (Erickson, 1992). Because contextual circumstances always vary from setting to setting, it is simply impossible for a researcher to provide accurate judgments about the extent to which his or her findings might be generalized to other situations. Even in quasi-experimental studies—with large, randomly-selected samples—researchers can only speak of averages and general tendencies, not specific applications from one case to another. Ultimately, however, in the field of education, it is individual cases with which we are most concerned.

Drawing upon the language of Piaget's schema theory—with terms such as assimilation, accommodation, integration, and differentiation—Donmoyer (1990) argues that reading a single case can provide us with a vicarious experience which we can then transfer to other situations in our own lives. Case studies can expand our horizons by taking us to distant or exotic places where we may not otherwise be able to go. Few people would deny that books and stories have this power. For example, in reading Tolstoy's *Childhood, Boyhood, and Youth*, I traveled back in time—to Russia in the 1830s and 1840s—and emerged with a rich understanding of what it was like to be a young aristocrat in that particular time and place. Reading case studies also enables us to see the world from another person's point of view. They enrich our understanding of a phenomenon by allowing us to experience it from a perspective that is different from our own. For instance, by reading Peshkin's (1986) study of a fundamentalist Christian school, I gained a unique insight into this phenomenon which I may not have otherwise experienced—even if I had visited the same school myself. In addition, we are more likely to learn from vicarious experiences because they tend to be less threatening than direct encounters. As Donmoyer notes, people often become defensive when they are challenged by new ideas or novel experiences. A teacher who reads a narrative account of the discipline problems faced by another teacher would likely feel less threatened than if he or she were initially asked to confront similar kinds of problems in his or her own classroom.

Generalizability has not traditionally been considered a strength of interpretive research—especially when the term has been narrowly defined as making extrapolations from a sample to population (Firestone, 1993). However, when the concept of generalizability is expanded to include the kind of understanding that occurs when we learn something in a particular situation and then apply it to similar situations, it is clear that interpretive research possesses a tremendous strength in this area that has hitherto been under-appreciated. Life history research in particular—with its narrative structure and literary quality—is especially well-suited for fostering this kind of learning.

PART III

STORIES OF ANNA

As I stated in the Prologue, my collaboration with Anna began in the context of a university course on qualitative research methods entitled, "Qualitative (Human Science) Approaches to Educational Research: A Focus on Ethnography." It was taught by Gary Knowles during the 1991-1992 academic year, spanning two full semesters. In the first semester, we explored the underlying assumptions of interpretive research as well as the designs and methods employed in various ethnographic studies, while in the second semester we each designed and conducted our own ethnographic study. For reasons that are explained in the Prologue, I chose to collaborate with Anna for my study. What were her beliefs about reading and writing? What were her teaching practices? How were these beliefs and practices related? These were the questions that initially motivated my inquiry.

In order to understand Anna's beliefs, I conducted two 2-hour interviews with her, which I audiotaped and transcribed. I also interviewed several of her friends and colleagues who had known her throughout her career—including a counselor and an assistant principal at her school and one of her former professors at the University of Michigan. These interviews, too, were audiotaped and transcribed. In addition, Anna provided me with copies of nearly two-dozen academic papers that she had written for various graduate-level university courses during the 1970s and 1980s. These papers provided me with glimpses into the ways that her thinking had changed and evolved over time.

In order to understand Anna's teaching practices, I visited her classroom 11 times during the early months of 1992, carefully observing her lessons and writing fieldnotes. My role varied from day to day, depending upon the circumstances. Sometimes, I was a participant observer—sitting among the students, joining in their conversations, and helping them with their work—while other times, I sat by myself and quietly observed the class proceedings, always ready to join in whenever my participation seemed appropriate. I stopped going to Anna's classroom at the conclusion of Gary's course but resumed 17 months later when I decided to extend the study.

Thus, my research with Anna occurred in two distinct phases. The first phase, which spanned from January through April, 1992, occurred in the context of the course, while the second phase, which began in September, 1993, lasted until Anna retired from teaching in 1998. In the chapters that follow I utilize data collected during both phases of my work.

In Chapter 5, I provide an overview of Anna's life. It is by no means a comprehensive account, for my goal was not to delve deeply into her personal life or to explore every facet of her career. Rather, my goal was simply to provide a general sense of who she was, where she came from, and how her life evolved—especially her life as a teacher. To accomplish this goal, I relied heavily upon our transcribed interviews and utilized Anna's own words as much as possible in the text that I crafted. I also drew from a variety of archival data—such as books, newspapers, and school yearbooks—in order to illuminate some of the important social, political, and historical contexts in which Anna's life has been situated. Providing this kind of information is what distinguishes a life *history* from a life *story.* A life history is a life story in context.

In Chapter 6, I analyze Anna's current teaching practices and the underlying beliefs that guided them. Her beliefs—which included beliefs about literacy, beliefs about teaching, and beliefs about students—fell into two broad categories. First, there were transitory beliefs, which were shaped largely by her school-related experiences as a student and as a preservice teacher, and second, there were enduring beliefs that were predominantly rooted in her basic life experiences outside school. Over time Anna either abandoned or reshaped many of her transitory beliefs while drawing heavily upon her core of more enduring beliefs in order to create a functional pedagogy.

CHAPTER 5

ANNA'S LIFE HISTORY

It was Thursday, March 5, 1992, when I conducted my first formal interview with Anna. I had already visited her classroom several times and knew what she did there. Now, I wanted to learn more about her background as a teacher—including her beliefs about reading and writing and the life experiences that helped to shape them. The interview took place at Anna's house, a brand-new condominium that she had recently purchased. Greeting me at the door and leading me into the dining room, she laughingly remarked that I was one of the first official visitors to her new home. She then gave me a brief tour before leading me into the dining room.

Anna is not an easy person to describe. Quiet, modest, and unassuming, she is not a self-promoter. She does not relish attention. She would much rather be characterized as an ordinary teacher who has spent her career fumbling around trying to make things work, than as an expert who has all the answers. Genuinely embarrassed when talking about herself, she is difficult to know. I have spent many months working with her—years even—yet she has always remained an enigma to me in some ways.

On the surface, there is nothing extraordinary about Anna. She comes across as calm, good-natured, and easygoing, with a self-effacing sense of humor that sometimes causes people to underestimate her. When she speaks, Anna often punctuates her sentences with soft laughter, especially when the conversation is about her. In talking about her teaching, she evokes an image not unlike the classic television episode of *I Love Lucy* in which Lucy and Ethel get jobs in a chocolate factory (Oppenheimer, Carroll, & Pugh, 1952). Their assignment is to wrap each piece of candy as it goes by on a conveyer belt. The task is manageable at first, but the machine gradually speeds up, forcing the two women to stuff excess candy into their mouths, hats, and blouses in a vain attempt to keep pace. I think Anna sometimes sees her work as a teacher as being similar to Lucy and Ethel in the chocolate factory—trying to keep pace in a world where the conveyer belt is continually speeding up.

Beneath this self-effacing exterior, however, lies a person with a formidable intellect—someone who is passionate about literature, poetry, and the written word and who has dedicated her life to their study. Anna reminds me of my late grandmother in this regard. Like my grandmother, Anna is a lover of books, a lover of ideas, and she has lived her life in pursuit of this passion. Over the years, she has focused a great deal of her energy on teaching and scholarly interests. In addition to teaching English at Windrow High School during the daytime, she also teaches in the school's night program a couple of days a week, and she serves on various curriculum committees throughout the school year. During the summer, she coordinates a regional conference for adult writers in Michigan. In her spare time, she is working on a Ph.D. in English Education. Anna sometimes jokes that she has no social life, but she actually has a rich social life—one that is filled with the kinds of activities that she truly loves.

While I was setting up my audiotape recorder on Anna's dining room table and arranging a large pile of papers that I wanted to discuss, Anna was in the kitchen preparing a pot of tea. "I've been looking forward to this interview," she said, returning to the dining room. "This whole experience has been so enlightening to me. The odd thing is that reflecting on my work is *not* something that I don't do anyway."

"But you usually don't do it with someone else, do you?" I asked, sipping from the cup of hot tea that she had just poured.

"No, not with someone else and not in such a formal way," she replied. "You know, instead of just going back through my old papers and looking for ideas, I've started to look at how things have developed. And I wouldn't do that self-consciously." Anna paused to pour her own cup of tea while I hastily checked my tape recorder to make sure it was still running. Then, continuing, she said, "But I've always cared about what I think and how I came to think the way I do...."

Throughout the ensuing conversation—and the many that followed—Anna and I discussed topics ranging from her conceptions of reading and writing, to her approach to students, to her feelings about schooling and education in general. We also discussed elements of her life history, such as her family and early school experiences, her decision to become a teacher, and the evolution of her career as an educator. In this chapter, I draw upon these conversations and other information to present my version of Anna's life history.

Childhood

Reading and writing always played an important role in Anna's life. Growing up in a rural community in Southeastern Michigan, she was always surrounded by adults who valued literacy. "I learned to write before I even went to school," she said.

> I remember writing, sitting alongside my father when he was in graduate school and I was in kindergarten and modeling with nonsense words, copying things. And there would be quiet times in the evening where I would sit with a book or magazine at three and four before I could read, just to be with the adults.

Anna described her home as being fairly typical of white middle class America in the post-World War II era. It was a closeknit family with four children—three boys and one girl. Both of her parents came from immigrant families, and her grandparents lived next door. The only thing that she considered to be unusual was the fact that her mother's parents could not read or write. "School wasn't any part of their experience," she said.

> They had left the Old Country—Poland and Russia—and come to this country and started to work at the Ford Motor Company. They got to be middle class people by virtue of work, not education.... They understood the value of education, but from a very different point of view than the people around me who took education for granted.

Anna fondly remembered the role that her mother played in helping her grandparents to communicate with their relatives still living in Europe.

> [My mother] was always writing letters for them to the Old
> Country and reading the letters that came. She was bilingual.
> She could speak both English and Polish—and some Ger-
> man—and she would translate the letters. Those would be
> events. We would sit around the table, and Grandma and
> Grandpa would come. We would picture the lives of these
> people we'd never met and probably never would.

Anna's early interest in reading and writing was reinforced by her
school experiences. She remembered, "In grade school, I had exceptional
language arts teachers. As I look back now we did a lot of reading, and
we were encouraged to read and write outside the class." Anna attended a
small Catholic school that was run by four nuns, each of whom taught
two classes with mixed grades. "Having two grades in one room," she
explained, "you always knew what to anticipate for the next year because
you saw exactly what was going to happen. And I was a kid who was a
fast finisher, always eager to move on to the next reader." Indeed, Anna
said that she always excelled in text-oriented activities.

> We had classroom contests, out-of-school contests, all kinds
> of writing contests, and I was always encouraged to enter
> because I always did fairly well. It was something that I felt
> accomplished at and enjoyed doing…. I really saw it as a
> source of identity as a student.

Anna continued her interest in academic pursuits as a student at a
small, private high school for girls—and later when she was in college.
In describing her high school, she said:

> It drew students from the metropolitan Detroit area. I lived
> about twenty miles from the school, so all the activities that I
> did were during school hours. We didn't have after-school
> activities. We didn't have sports teams, so it wasn't like a
> typical high school in that sense. There were boarders too. I
> wasn't a boarder, but there were residential students in the
> school.

Within this environment, Anna found it relatively easy to establish friend-
ships with other students who shared her scholarly interests.

My circle of friends weren't from the same town. We were all from either rural communities or from the city, but none of us were from the town where the school was located. We traveled to get there, and that sort of drew us together.... I remember having what I would consider pseudo-intellectual conversations about issues, such as when Kennedy was a candidate, and when the Beatles were a big deal. It was also a Catholic institution, and there were a lot of changes going on in the Church at that time, so I had some awareness of a bigger world, which has been useful to me. I think my mind was opened rather early to other possibilities.

Anna also credited her parents—her father in particular—with instilling in her a sense of critical inquisitiveness about the world, and a sense of social responsibility. Her father was an attorney whom she described as being "a practical man," someone for whom practicing law was more of a means for social benefit than a means for personal enrichment. "He was a strong people's advocate and did things that I can admire now, but which I didn't understand as a youngster. We didn't get rich and famous," she said with a laugh. Further describing her father, she said:

He didn't see law as a way to self-promote. He was always very proud of being a Democrat in a Republican town and being one of the few Democrats in his Republican law school class. He had a very populist sense and a very pragmatic sense of what an education meant. He knew that he was providing better for his family than his father had been able to do. But he was never interested in social mobility. In fact, he would often introduce himself to people as a farmer.

Anna laughed when she remembered how her father used to look through her history book or some other school assignment and remark that she was not being truly educated—that the sisters didn't know what they were talking about. "That created a tension in me," she said, with her laughter fading into a soft smile.

I wanted to be a good student. I wanted to do everything the sisters were telling us.... Had my mother not been one who encouraged more conformity, he would have been one to say, "Tell her she doesn't know what the Constitution says. You're learning this and it's really not that." In some ways, as I think back, that was helpful.

College

After graduating from high school in 1964, Anna enrolled at Michigan State University in East Lansing. In college, she hoped to encounter a thriving community of scholars—people with whom she could share and expand her intellectual interests. What she found, however, was very different. "I was surprised that students weren't as serious-minded as I thought they were going to be," she said.

> I had anticipated college as being kind of like high school but just more intense. Yet when I got there, I found that I had to really seek out people who were interested in academics. That puzzled me. I was really disoriented for a while.

Anna gradually overcame this feeling of isolation and confusion by pursuing extracurricular activities that involved reading and writing. She served as an editor for the literary magazine; she attended poetry readings; and she actively sought out professors and other individuals who shared her passion for the written word.

During this time, Anna's career options wavered among several professions, including teaching and journalism. "I knew in elementary school that teaching was important to me," she said.

> But I also knew that writing was something I wanted to do. I had considered journalism but wasn't sure that I liked that kind of writing. I didn't like writing under pressure. Writing was always a leisure sort of activity for me. It was something I enjoyed doing slowly, deliberately. And having worked on school newspapers and such, I knew that journalism was a pressure situation. I didn't like that kind of writing.

Anna ultimately decided to become a teacher, although she explained that her decision was motivated more by pragmatic concerns than by any special calling that she felt to the profession.

> I had started school as just a liberal arts major—an English major—and I wasn't in the teaching track and didn't begin to

take education courses until my junior year. I think it was a
question of wanting to support myself.... I wanted to be independent, so teaching was a practical move so I could be
financially independent.

After committing herself to this career choice, Anna decided that she
wanted to do her student teaching in Detroit. "I knew I wanted to work in
a city," she explained. "I didn't want small-town living.... I thought of
the city as an important place where all the world's work was done."
Having just read Daniel Fader's *Hooked on Books* (Fader, 1966), Anna
hoped to student teach at Northwestern High School, which was one of
the schools that Fader mentioned as having used his program.[16] However, this placement never materialized. "I don't know how the assignments were made, but I was sent to Windrow instead. I was disappointed
at first, but then I met my supervising teacher, and I was delighted with
the school."

Windrow in the 1960s

Windrow was still relatively new in 1967 when Anna did her student
teaching. Built a decade earlier as a neighborhood school with an initial
enrollment of approximately 900 students, it had been expanded in the
early 1960s to meet the needs of a growing community. "Windrow is now
a small school," the 1961 yearbook stated. "It is a close school, a tight
school." Continuing in sentimental language that evokes an idealized
image of social harmony and blithe contentment, the yearbook said:

There is no prevailing division of classes, no extensive social discrimination.... There is freedom at Windrow, more
'subtle' liberty. Here, one usually finds escape from classroom restrictions at lunch or class exchange: for at Windrow
there is no frantic hurry through the halls, no over-jammed
lunchrooms inspiring disgust and indigestion. At best, we are
a somewhat leisurely lot....

The student photographs included row after row of clean-cut smiling young
faces, with the boys dressed in coats and ties and the girls wearing dresses
and necklaces—all of them looking so innocent and blissfully unaware of
the tumultuous years that lay just a few years ahead... civil rights... Vietnam... student protests... riots in the cities....

The following year, 1962, as astronaut John Glenn was exciting the nation with his journey into space, Windrow High School was in the midst of a major building expansion. Capturing the excitement of the times, a yearbook writer compared the impending building project to a space flight—his prose suggesting an unwavering faith in science and a naively optimistic vision of the future.

> Space scientists watching a successful rocket leave the pad could not be happier than the students, parents, faculty, and guests who attended the ceremony were as they saw their dreams begin to materialize. Just as the world changes in many significant ways after a major scientific breakthrough, so will Windrow change in many aspects other than physical after its completion. This September will witness an increase in sports and extra-curricular activities, new and challenging courses, a single-session class schedule, a population explosion, and an increase in city-wide respect and recognition.

By 1967, Windrow's enrollment had almost tripled. With more than 3000 students and 130 teachers, it had become one of the largest high schools in the city, and was widely regarded as a model institution. The Report of Findings and Recommendations of the Detroit High School Study (High School Study Commission, 1967) called the building "an excellent example of a well-constructed school edifice" (p. 7). At that time, it served a predominantly white, middle class community with approximately three percent of the students being African-American. Sixty-eight percent of the 1967 graduates applied to college, up from 52 percent in 1960, and the report praised the faculty for their excellent work—especially in the areas of math, English, science, and music. In addition, race relations were reported to be excellent, with African-American students and members of ethnic minorities being well-integrated into the school community. Their achievement patterns, it stated, mirrored those of the larger student body.[17]

Walkout at Northern High School

In many ways, the scenario at Windrow in the 1960s represented the calm before the storm. By 1967, some Detroit schools were already experiencing the racial tensions that had gripped the nation at large. In April,

1966, for instance, there was a massive student protest at Northern High School. More than 2300 students at the predominantly African-American school staged a walkout in protest of the principal's decision to ban the publication of an uncomplimentary editorial in the school newspaper. Written by a white honor student, the editorial maintained that students who graduated from Northern and other predominantly African-American schools in the Detroit system were not adequately prepared for college and the workplace. "We simply do not feel that such a drastic difference in classroom achievement, such as the one between Redford (a predominantly white school in Detroit) and Northern, should be allowed to exist," the editorial was quoted as saying (Mackey, 1966, p. 1A). "We don't believe that students should pass any class for any other reason than having completed the course satisfactorily" (pp. 1A, 4A). The editorial went on to suggest that a uniform test be administered to all prospective graduates of Detroit's high schools in order to ensure that they had met a minimum standard of academic achievement.

Defending his decision to censor the editorial, the principal maintained that he did not regularly read student editorials in advance, but that when the author interviewed him about conditions in the school, he "was so anti-everything (that) I told the head of the department that he had better take a look at the article before it was published" (Mackey, 1966, p. 4A). The department head agreed with the principal and supported the editorial's censorship—which rapidly escalated into a major incident. With the backing of many of the school's teachers, as well as support from a local civil rights organization, the editorial writer and several of his classmates staged a walkout that ultimately involved the entire student body and some of the parents. It was a peaceful event that seemed to be accompanied by a festive spirit. A large photograph featured on the front page of the *Detroit Free Press* (Plofchan, 1966) showed a sizable group of student protesters—many of them with smiles on their faces—milling around the school.

The pleasant demeanors of these demonstrators, however, did not mask their determination to bring about change. Parading around the building and down the street to a large neighborhood church, the crowd held a brief rally and read a list of demands. These included the removal of the principal, the removal of an unpopular police officer who was permanently assigned to the building, and the gathering of comparative data on the academic standards at Detroit's other high schools in order to create a plan for improving the quality of education at Northern. The superintendent of the Detroit Public Schools immediately acquiesced to the second demand and removed the police officer, but he delayed in making decisions regarding the other two. Later, however, a special committee was formed to assess the conditions in all of the city's public high schools. The Detroit High School Study of 1967, with its glowing report on the conditions at Windrow, resulted from the work of this committee.

Shortly after the protest at Northern, which was viewed favorably in an editorial that appeared in the *Detroit Free Press* ("One Protest," 1966), the newspaper published a scathing expose on the poor conditions in other Detroit public schools. Sending one of its reporters into a predominantly African-American junior high school under the guise of being a substitute teacher, the *Free Press* printed a four-part story that told of crumbling buildings, shortages of books, and teacher indifference (Treloar, 1966a, 1966b, 1966c, 1966d). In describing the classroom to which he was assigned, the reporter wrote:

> There was a wad of gum stuck on the blackboard. In one corner, paint flaked off the ceiling. Later, students would sit very still and watch the pieces drift down and land on their shoulders and in their hair, artificial dandruff.
>
> I don't know how old the desks were, but there must have been two generations of initials etched into the unvarnished tops. Each desk had a hole for an inkwell, and those were going out of date when I was in school.
>
> There's a dark little courtyard just outside the window with iron gratings everywhere. In the middle sat a cement something where trash was thrown.
>
> Miss Schaal (the head of the English department) saw me looking out the window. "We had lovely curtains to cover the window, but the last teacher in this room took them. She only lasted five months" (Treloar, 1966a, p. 1A).

The reporter continued by explaining the school's textbook policy as it was related to him by Miss Schaal.

> "The seventh and eighth graders don't GET textbooks," she said.
>
> "When I get them to you, the books are to be kept in the room. You pass them out when you need them, and you col-

lect them at the end of the hour. If the children took books home, we'd never get them back.

"The ninth graders will get English texts, but they'll have to sign out for them. We try to push homework on the ninth graders, but don't bank on it ever getting done" (Treloar, 1966a, p. 10A).

In a later installment, the reporter elaborated on the negative attitude that permeated the teaching staff:

Instead of dealing with the problem of attitudes, a third to a half of Jefferson's teachers have rejected their students as "uneducable."

For the new teachers fresh out of college, there is plenty of encouragement to "give up."

When he doesn't do well on the first few days, there are embittered teachers on every side ready to tell him: "These kids are just plain dumb. You will never teach them anything...."

Friday morning, my last day at Jefferson, I walked up the front steps with one of the new teachers, a young man just graduated from Michigan State University.

I asked him how he felt after his first week in a new profession.

"It's one week toward retirement," he shrugged (Treloar, 1966c, pp. 1A, 8A).

The incident at Northern, followed by this shocking series of newspaper articles, highlighted the poor quality of education that was afforded to minority students in Detroit. It also highlighted the racial tensions that had long existed within the city, and, in retrospect, perhaps foreshadowed the massive riot that consumed Detroit in the summer of 1967.[18]

Student Teaching at Windrow

As parts of Detroit burned in 1967, the neighborhoods surrounding Windrow were largely unaffected. There were no lootings, no arrests, and no injuries or deaths. Life immediately after the riot continued much as it had before. During the next several years, however, there was a notable rise in the white flight to the suburbs that had begun in the 1950s. In

1946, for example, more than 80 percent of the students in the city's schools were white, while by 1967 this percentage had dwindled to 40. Eight years later it was less than 23 percent (Mirel, 1993). The statistics at Windrow followed this general trend during the 1970s and 1980s, although the school was almost entirely unintegrated before 1970. A former high-ranking administrator in the Detroit Public Schools, with whom I spoke, explained the transition in this way:

> The Detroit Public School population had about a two-percent change every year from white to black, from about 1960 when we started counting it until it leveled off at about 88 percent black, which would have been in the late '70s or early '80s. And that change had a slight bump in it, maybe three percent or four percent, during the year or two when the desegregation plan went in in 1975 and 1976. But there was a very small bump at that point. It was almost a straight line of two percent change per year, and the area around Windrow High School was a typical example of an all-white community which during that time went from all-white to what is probably now, I would guess, between 80 percent and 90 percent black.

The setting in which Anna did her student teaching was the pre-1970 version of Windrow High School. Working with a mentor teacher whom she described as being "traditional" in her pedagogy, Anna taught two tenth-grade English classes and received a good evaluation. "Miss Henson is most pleasant and cooperative," wrote her mentor teacher on the official evaluation form. "She has a friendly, relaxed but not permissive manner with her students… which create(s) an atmosphere conducive to learning." Continuing, the teacher wrote:

> [Anna] is extremely well prepared in her field in subject matter material as well as methodology and techniques. She has planned and presented some excellent lessons, showing initiative and creativity in bringing in relevant resource materials and making good use of visual aids…. I have the highest regard for Miss Henson's personal and professional qualities. She does not resist criticism and shows genuine interest and concern for her students. I believe she will be a fine teacher.

After graduating from Michigan State, Anna interviewed for several teaching positions in Detroit and nearby Lansing—but had difficulty in finding a job. "This was in the late '60s when the profession was pretty much saturated," she explained. "With Vietnam, there were a lot more males applying for positions as teachers." She was eventually hired as a substitute teacher in Lansing, where she filled in for absent teachers at all grade levels. In describing this experience, she said:

> I was very uncomfortable with the uncertainty of not know-
> ing what grade level I would teach from day to day. I subbed
> in elementary classrooms, as well as high school classrooms,
> and I learned quickly that I was uncomfortable with little bitty
> kids. I just felt that the days were endless when I was as-
> signed to an elementary classroom. I didn't know what to do
> with all these little kids who didn't know what to do [laugh-
> ing].

In addition to her job as a substitute teacher, Anna enrolled in graduate school at Michigan State, and she also worked in a nursing home as a caregiver for the elderly. Years earlier, she had assumed this same role in her own family. Her mother had a heart condition and was an invalid from the time Anna was thirteen years old until she died when Anna was twenty-six, so Anna was largely responsible not only for her mother but for her three younger brothers as well. Later, Anna also cared for her elderly grandmother, who lived with her before she died.

Beginning Teacher

While living and working in Lansing, Anna received an unexpected job offer from the Detroit Public Schools—teaching English to seventh-, eighth-, and ninth-graders. She jumped at this opportunity and reported to work on the Monday before Thanksgiving in 1969. By all accounts, this was a very difficult experience for Anna. The teacher whom she re-placed was an alcoholic who had been released for drinking on the job, and the classroom she inherited was in a state of chaos. "I remember asking the principal if he at least had a list of names, so that I'd have a place to begin," she said, "but he said 'no.' He just walked me to the classroom and closed the door. I will never forget that."

For Anna, teaching at Franklin Junior High was not at all like student teaching at Windrow—or subbing in Lansing. Instead, it was much more similar to the experience that Treloar (1966a, 1966b, 1966c, 1966d) had described in his series of articles in the *Detroit Free Press*. Anna explained it as follows:

> Franklin was in a state of transition. When I got there, it was no longer a school that had lots of parental support and a strong staff with strong leadership. New teachers were starting to come in, while the experienced ones were leaving. They were simply not ready for the kinds of things that they were beginning to see in the classroom. And, typical of a school in transition, the leadership began to retire, so we just didn't get the right kind of support. There was this sort of flailing around looking for ways to keep going…. By the time I left the school seven years later, 95 percent of the staff had changed. That's an amazing turnover.

One of Anna's colleagues at this school remembered Anna as a teacher who got off to a very rough start—an assessment with which Anna readily agreed:

> I had so much trouble at first. And I was so disappointed. I was young and enthusiastic and couldn't wait to get into the classroom—and then to have all of this resistance addressed at me personally was extremely disappointing…. The kids were vicious—the things they wrote and the things they said. I remember that there was just this overwhelming sense that I wasn't wanted there, and nowhere in my wildest imagination had I ever pictured myself being the object of that kind of hostility…. I mean rowdiness and that kind of thing I was ready for, but I was totally unprepared for these kinds of personal attacks. Sometimes, I'd stay out in the parking lot for a half-hour in tears before I could drive home, wondering how in the world I was going to walk back in there the next day with any kind of dignity.

Anna told this story with a faint smile on her face, as if she could hardly believe her own inexperience, and she was very frank in discussing her shortcomings. "Part of the problem," she explained, "was that I kept appealing to the whole class."

> I can say now, with some experience, that I wasn't looking at
> the class as a group of individuals, except for the tormentors,
> except for the leaders. And at the same time, I was ignoring
> the other kids who would have been great allies. I just kept
> appealing to the whole class....

With the help of some of her colleagues, Anna was gradually able to
move beyond this rough beginning and establish a niche for herself at
Franklin, much as she had done in college. "Things did pick up," she
said, "thanks to the support of people who saw that I was in trouble and
cared enough about the kids and about me to help." Indeed, Anna's first-
year performance evaluation, which was a simple checklist completed by
her principal, contained "good" or "superior" ratings in every category.

Anna, however, was not satisfied. In searching for solutions to the
problems that she encountered in her classroom, she enrolled in graduate
school at the University of Michigan, which involved a shorter commute
from Detroit than Michigan State, and she began to work on a Master of
Arts degree in education. In explaining her thinking at the time, she said:

> My expectations of students when I started teaching were
> very traditional. I thought that I was responsible for bringing
> the work to them, that they were to take in all the things that
> I had been prepared to teach. Of course, that fell apart really
> quickly. Nothing that I learned in my teacher education pro-
> gram prepared me for kids who didn't read, couldn't read,
> and were struggling with the simplest tasks in writing—like
> writing names. I didn't see how anything I was prepared to
> do fit the requirements of the job. So that lack of fit made me
> begin to question and draw from other resources for how to
> do this, how to make this work. My initial conflict was some-
> thing that drove me back to school.... I thought that there
> must be some way an M.A. in education would answer some
> questions for me on things that I wasn't getting help with
> within the system.

One of Anna's professors from that time remembered her as being a
quiet student. It wasn't that she didn't participate," he explained to me
during an interview.

But she had a kind of held back, soft, reserved demeanor that made it necessary for me as a teacher to draw her out. And already, it was my practice in those days to get to know the stories of my students, get a sense of who they were, what their major life concerns were as well as their more academic interests. So, it soon became clear to me that Anna was deeply involved in her teaching of English, that she cared a lot about her students, but she was quite diffident about her ability to reach them.

One problem was that Anna felt trapped by the official English curriculum at Franklin Junior High, which consisted primarily of the *Robert's English* textbook (Roberts, 1968) with a heavy emphasis on transformational grammar. On one hand, she felt obligated to follow this curriculum, while on the other hand, she knew it was not working. "I knew that kids sitting with that old *Roberts English Series* book in seventh and eighth grade and writing out those transformational grammar sentences was not (productive)," she said.

> (The book) had nothing to do with the students. It had very little to do with me. The writing that the students were doing was just reproducing what was in the textbooks, completely remote from their lives. They had little interest in writing it, and I had little interest in reading it, so we weren't making any connection at all.

Nevertheless, Anna continued to receive favorable evaluations from her supervisors. A second-year evaluation conducted by her department head included the following narrative description of one of her lessons:

> Two pictures, each containing many errors and discrepancies, were projected on the overhead projector. Pupils were to list at least five errors for each. Discussion revealed that not all students had the same answers since people see things differently. The last few minutes of the class were spent with crossword puzzles.

The department head also noted that Anna had difficulty in getting the students to cooperate during the discussion but he praised her efforts nonetheless.

> Miss Henson tried hard to get students to participate in an
> orderly manner in the discussion. Unfortunately, many have
> not yet learned to raise their hands and be recognized. I find
> this typical of many of our students and I do not feel that this
> is because of any negligence on Miss Henson's part.

Each year, Anna's official evaluations became more and more com-
plimentary of her teaching, showing a steady progression in her performance—at least as it was perceived by her supervisors. Her third-year
evaluation stated that Anna "began the class promptly after the tardy bell,"
and instructed her students to silently read the explanatory material while
she took attendance. Continuing, it said:

> The several students who were tardy were quickly and qui-
> etly given their instructions with a minimum of disturbance
> to the rest of the class. When Miss Henson began to work
> orally with the class, most students were attentive and seemed
> to get the point of the lesson.

The evaluation concluded with the observation that Anna's classroom was
"neat and attractive." The next year, the department head commented not
only on the appearance of Anna's room, but on the atmosphere as well,
writing, "The classroom is decorated with many colorful posters and seems
a pleasant place to be."

By now, Anna had begun to move beyond the confines of the official
school curriculum, with its emphasis on transformational grammar, and
she began to design her own curriculum around the needs and interests of
her students. She said:

> I began to draw on more community resource type things. I
> worked with the *Bulletin Spirits* program and brought bulle-
> tins to my classroom. We (the students) did writing in the
> bulletin; we made little books; we did all that stuff that whole
> language is describing now. We were doing this then. I took
> lots of pictures of the kids and activities in the classroom and
> then asked them to think about them and write about that....
> It was essentially a combined curriculum—the things the
> school provided and the things I was trying to provide.

In spite of her apparent successes as a teacher, deep inside, Anna remained dissatisfied with her job and seriously considered pursuing another career. "I thought I probably wasn't going to be a very effective teacher and that if I wanted to do something useful, then I should think about getting out of the classroom," she said. "But I was mostly burned out. I didn't feel like I had the energy or the resources left. Even though I could figure out ways of making it work, I couldn't see myself doing this for another 20 years." Therefore, Anna began to apply for various administrative jobs that were posted in the school district. "The school secretary would pay attention to all the vacancies and openings for positions downtown and would recommend stuff for me," Anna explained. "She would tell me, 'You should apply for that,' 'You should do this,' 'You should get on this committee....' I knew that she knew the system inside and out, and that if she recommended it, then I should do it."

One position for which Anna applied was Junior Administrative Assistant in the Publications Department of the Detroit Public Schools. The Publications Department was responsible for generating the various forms that were used by teachers and administrators throughout the school district. Anna made it past the first interview and was given a packet to take home and complete as part of the next phase of the screening process. The packet included several assignments similar to the kinds of tasks that she would be required to do in this position. One assignment asked her to redesign the school district's "Subject Progress Report" form. "It's the same one we're still using today," Anna said, as she flipped through a stack of papers that she pulled from an old manila folder. The instructions were very detailed:

> Examine the attached Form 1014, "Subject Progress Report." Then, draw-up in pencil an improved version of this form, keeping in mind the needs of those who must fill it out (school teachers and counselors) and those at the receiving end (parents of high-school students) who must understand and apply the information. Clean erasures are acceptable in your drawing. Retain the 8 1/2 x 11" size. Do not specify type faces or sizes—merely hand-print large or small, and suggest rule-thicknesses by the lightness or heaviness of pencil-lines. You are allowed to revise the wording if you think best, but keep it simple. If you have to make some doubtful assumptions, attach a statement.

Anna showed me the tentative drawing that she produced in response to this rather intimidating prompt. "I didn't have a clue what to do," she laughingly exclaimed. "I think that's when I stopped wanting to be an administrator."

Anna taught at Franklin Junior High for a few more years before finally making a radical career change. Taking a leave of absence from her job, she abruptly moved to Oregon and enrolled in graduate school at Portland State University. In explaining her rationale behind this decision, Anna said that she did not leave her job because she was particularly unhappy at that time in her career. "It's just that I was getting completely overwhelmed by the kinds of problems that kids were bringing to school," she said. "I simply knew that I needed to get away and needed time to think, and I thought that a different place would help me to make some decisions—away from school, away from family."

The specific event that immediately precipitated Anna's departure from Detroit was the decision of the school district to convert Franklin Junior High into a middle school. This meant that the school would consist of grades 6-8 instead of 7-9, and Anna would have to obtain additional certification in order to teach the new sixth-graders; she was not eager to do this. "My interest had always been with the older kids," she said.

> I had taught eighth- and ninth-graders and occasionally seventh, but found seventh grade really tedious. The kids were just too active and not as intellectually engaged as the older kids. They needed so much emotional support that I just felt exhausted, emotionally exhausted. I also had an interest in my subject matter, and I had looked forward to teaching in high school eventually. I mean that was my original plan when I first started teaching.

Since no high school English positions were available for Anna, she decided to leave Michigan and travel west to Oregon. Taking a one-year sabbatical from teaching and re-enrolling in graduate school—this time away from the familiar setting of Michigan in which she had spent her entire life—she was able to fully immerse herself in the kinds of scholarly activities that had always appealed to her. She grew a great deal during this time, both personally and professionally. "That was a really valuable year in a lot of ways," she said. "I studied American Literature and did quite a bit of thinking about teaching, and I came back with resolve that that was what I wanted to do." Although Anna had gone to Oregon with no firm commitment to return to Michigan, she soon decided that Portland was not the kind of city where she wanted to live permanently. "Portland seemed to be about twenty years behind the rest of the country," she explained.

> It was not a very progressive place politically. The pace was so different (from Detroit), and I wasn't particularly comfortable there.... So I wrote back to Detroit and told the personnel director that if he could find me a high school English position, I'd be happy to come back.

Return to Windrow

Coincidentally, there happened to be an opening at Windrow High School, the same school where she had student-taught ten years earlier. The school, however, had undergone many changes. In fact, the entire city had changed. The 1970s was a tumultuous decade for Detroit (Mirel, 1993). Between 1970 and the 1980, it lost more than one-fifth of its population, as white middle class families steadily fled to the suburbs. Businesses, too, deserted the city at an alarming rate, which further drained the already-diminished tax base upon which the schools depended for their funding. Thus, teachers found themselves in the difficult position of encountering an increasing number of poor and minority students while their resources were simultaneously being cut. By 1977, when Anna returned to Windrow, almost three-quarters of the students were African-American. Nine years later, it was almost totally segregated, with virtually no white students remaining.

In spite of the turmoil associated with this transition, Anna began her new job at Windrow with a great deal of enthusiasm. "I thought after seven years of making due at Franklin—just trying to get by—I was finally going to be able to do all those things that they taught me about in college," she said. "I was going to present the curriculum, the college-bound curriculum. Wrong!" Her excitement quickly faded when she discovered that none of her classes were in the college-bound track. "My first semester at Windrow, I had five remedial classes," she said. "They were RC classes, which meant 'Reading Comprehension.' It was a dry compensatory reading program that included lots of pages—lots of standing at the ditto machine, which is something that I absolutely refused to do."

Just as she had done at Franklin, Anna began to look for ways to transcend the prescribed curriculum to which she felt bound, and she turned to writing as a way to engage her students. "We spent more class time writing than we did reading—and working from their texts," she explained. She also turned to the students themselves and listened to their concerns.

> I started looking at what kids cared about when they came to class, and it usually had nothing to do with how creative my dittos were or what wonderful magazines I was bringing in. It had to do with each other. They cared about who was showing up each day. How that had escaped me all those years I'll never know, but the kids were interested in the kids. But it never said that in any textbook. No one had ever told me that this was the kind of thing I should be looking at or working toward—creating some kind of cohesiveness among the group and trying to get the students to create the need to be there for each other.

During one of our tape-recorded interviews, Anna explained how this realization gradually transformed her teaching.

> We had a core group of kids—Jason, Robert, Mary, Duane.... I'll never forget those kids. They were so good to each other— so supportive. And I was simply honest with them that I didn't know exactly what we were going to do—only that we were going to try to work toward making the class enjoyable. I said, "You guys help me figure out how to do that."" And they were so creative and so original and so ambitious for each other in the kinds of things they suggested. They started telling me things like, "We need to talk. We need to have discussions in class about what we care about."
>
>   "Okay," I said, "you guys set this up. How are you going to do it? Who's in charge?" And I just sat back and let it happen and watched these kids start creating a class in a way that I had never been able to do. And there was this shift from my taking the whole responsibility for planning, for making it work, for content, for doing the things that I felt the teacher was being paid to do, to this sort of sharing the responsibility

for making things work. And, believe it or not, things started to work. We brought their lives into the classroom…and that has been an unforgettable class for me because they taught me my shortcomings as a planner.

Those kids stayed with me a year, and they seemed to almost adopt me as a teacher. They were very sensitive to my need for them to be successful in order for me to be satisfied somehow with the way things were working. And we could have these very candid conversations about why schools didn't work and why had they not been successful before. These were really bright kids, and here they were in this remedial class prepared to be put down, prepared to put each other down, but they somehow pulled together to show me that they could do things.

They were there every day. Their attendance didn't look anything like the attendance for my other remedial classes. Their grades didn't look anything like the grades for the other classes. You know, if a kid's not coming, there goes the grade! You simply have no other choice because attendance influences everything. There's also no cohesiveness in the class when the students aren't coming on a regular basis. There's no sense of community. And I have to say that this was the first class that I ever taught where I could characterize the group as having some communal sense, some sense of shared responsibility for one another. And we kept that. I was fortunate enough to have a number of these students back in the eleventh grade—this time in an Honor's class. They had worked their way out of the remedial track.

In telling this story, Anna emphasized that it took many more years for her to gain the ability and confidence to foster this kind of climate in her other classes. The transformation was gradual, she said, with this particular experience simply providing her with a glimpse into what a classroom might become—an ideal for which to strive.

Another experience that helped to shape the way Anna approached her students was teaching night school at Windrow, a practice which she began several years after starting her job there and which she continued until the program was cancelled in the mid-1990s. Acutely aware of the students who had failed in her class and ended up attending night school, Anna first became involved with this program in order to better understand the problem. "Teaching night school," she said, "I was forced to see students I had failed in ninth-grade or tenth-grade coming back to sit in the same room with the same teacher in the same building."

> I would have to ask myself, "How is it going to be different this time? What didn't work the first time? Who was responsible for this young person's failure?".... They would come back a little older, a little more mature, and I started to think that maturity is a part of learning. Maybe they simply weren't ready, and the things I was trying to do weren't for them at that time.... Kids' emotional maturity may be very different from their intellectual maturity. They may be ready to know something, but not to use it in the way I think it needs to be used. It started looking much more complex than I would have thought at an earlier time in my career when it was simply a question of, "Well, I gave you that assignment. You didn't do it."

In addition to teaching night classes, Anna also re-enrolled in graduate school at the University of Michigan and began to work on her doctoral degree in English Education. For Anna, taking college courses was always a way for her to engage herself intellectually and to think about her teaching, although she did not always see a direct connection between the university and her life as a teacher. While still at Franklin Middle School, for example, she felt an enormous gulf between what she was learning in education courses at the university and what she was experiencing in her classroom. She said:

> I initially took a lot of education courses thinking that my classroom experience, my classroom itself, would be relevant to things being discussed—and that simply wasn't the case. It wasn't just a case of obsessing on theory at the university; it was that practice was not very highly regarded.... But somehow, the things that I did learn at the university gave me some sense of affirmation that continuing with graduate school was the right choice—that I could enrich my practice and enrich my classroom and learn to value and reinforce values that I already had with education.

A Narrative Glimpse into
Anna's Classroom

The following vignette illustrates the general mood and tenor of Anna's classroom at Windrow High School as I experienced it during my visits. It depicts a particular instructional moment: a grading conference between Anna and one of her students.

•

"Are you going to read to me, Jackie?" Anna asked one of the three students who were seated next to her at a table in her classroom. It was a few minutes past 10:00 a.m., and I had walked into Anna's twelfth grade Honors English class just in time to see the beginning of a grading conference. Trying not to disrupt the conversation, I quietly sat down near the students and listened.

"Oh," the girl replied. "Do you want me to read it?"

"Yes, please," Anna said in an inviting tone.

With Anna and several other students seated around the table and listening attentively, Jackie began to read the essay that she had written in response to an assignment that was still printed on the chalkboard. The assignment was as follows:

> Write a persuasive essay convincing me of the grade you have earned. Consider your attendance, writing folder, vocabulary notebook, reading journal, use of class time, contributions to your group and class. Turn in a completed draft today.

"I feel that I should receive an *A* or an *A-*," Jackie said, with a trace of nervousness in her voice. "I feel it should be an *A* because I have good attendance, and my four freewrites are completed. I have done my book reviews and put forth all my hard work into them. I have one of my poems done, and the other two only need to be typed. I have 200 words in my vocabulary notebook. My attitude was very poor but I worked on it and my attitude has changed. Before I came to this class I was worried about my grade. But after talking to Ms. Henson, I realized that the grade wasn't important. It was what I had learned. Since the beginning of the year, I have made tremendous changes in the way I feel about working in groups and taking criticism from others. I feel that the lowest grade I should receive is an *A*- because all of my work is not completed. It will be completed by Friday. I put all of my effort into my work...."

Jackie concluded with a revelation about her attitude toward reading poetry in Anna's class. She said that she had hated it at first and had only recently begun to appreciate it. Then, looking up from her paper and momentarily making eye contact with Anna, she suddenly burst into laughter and looked away. "Don't look at me like that!" she said.

Anna laughed too and tried to put Jackie at ease "Don't look at you? Okay, I won't. How was I looking?"

"I don't know," Jackie replied, still laughing. "You're making me nervous."

"Don't be nervous, Jackie." Anna's voice was soft and reassuring. "We want to talk about it a little bit. You've written so much here. You did exactly what I asked you to do. I wanted you to consider all aspects of your work in here... And you've said something very similar to what Vivian[19] was just talking about. I don't expect that you'll just forget everything you've ever done in other classes, but I want you to think about things a little differently."

"I really didn't like it," Jackie said in reference to poetry. "If my other classes had had it, then I would have been prepared and wouldn't have a negative attitude toward it now. I wouldn't have thought like, 'Why do we have to have poetry? What is poetry going to do for you in the future?'"

"So you're getting more comfortable learning new things and putting them to use?" Anna asked. "I think that is a very accurate picture of Jackie today and yesterday."

Pointing at the *A* and *A*- written in Jackie's paper, Anna continued. "Now we have to decide between these two." This was the climax of the conference—the moment at which the grade was actually being assigned—and it was a particularly tense moment for both Anna and Jackie. Several weeks earlier, Anna's first grading conference with Jackie had been a disaster. Although I was not present to witness it first-hand, Anna had told me what happened.

"I said I thought the paper was worth a *B*. I turned to say, 'Jackie, what do you think?' But Jackie was gone! She flew to her seat and didn't come back. She showed no willingness to listen, or to talk it out, and I would have given her an opportunity to talk me into an *A* if she could have justified that to me. But she didn't even attempt that.... I tried to call her back that day to talk about it, but she was too impatient, and it was clear that that wasn't going to be the time."

In a very soft and consciously non-threatening voice, Anna now said to Jackie, "Do you think we have a little room to grow?"

"Yeah," Jackie replied.

"I think so too," said Anna. "...I think so too." She slowly wrote *A-* in her grade book while Jackie watched. Then, handing the essay back to Jackie, she smiled and said, "This goes back in your folder. Thanks for talking."

•

This brief description of a particular moment in Anna's classroom provides an important insight into what she valued as a teacher. For Anna, school was a place where students should be able to discover who they are and what they are good at. As early as 1974, she had written in a paper for a graduate course in education:

> I believe that education involves the total person; that an open mind and freedom to be oneself is a worthy goal. Personal growth, honesty, integrity, consistency, trust and love are as important to me professionally as they are personally. Developing dignity and character, and encouraging learning for its own sake are values that I hold for myself as well as for my students. Thus, the purpose of learning is to become more aware of oneself.

By encouraging Jackie to reflect on her work, Anna created an opening for her to begin to take measure of who she was. And, the Jackie who had walked away from her first conference in a rash display of impatience had gradually begun to look within herself and reflect on what she had seen. For Anna, it was through this kind of self-awareness and introspection that learning ultimately occurs. However, it was many years before she was able to put this belief into practice in her daily teaching. "I think overall the change was very slow and evolutionary," she said.

It probably started back with my own uncertainty way at the beginning of my career. But I stuck with a lot of bad teaching habits because I simply didn't feel able to make those changes. I was young and felt that I was responsible to a system, instead of responsible to children. I was an employee in this system that had a plan, and I believed that the plan was supposed to work. If I only worked hard enough, I could make it work. And students were sort of outside the equation. As a mature teacher, who can look a little differently at systems and feel much less responsible to the system than to the individual students who show up at the door, I know that by serving them, I am being responsible to the system. But there is little articulation on the system's part that says to me, "Teacher, you know what to do. Go ahead and do what's best." My sense was that I needed to follow the reading lists that kept us on certain pages at certain times of the year. That was the important thing—to keep up with the curriculum. And now I think of curriculum as a much bigger thing than page numbers and book titles. It is something that involves people. Students play a big role in shaping the curriculum....

CHAPTER 6

ANNA'S TEACHING PRACTICES
AND UNDERLYING BELIEFS

During the time I was visiting Anna's classroom, her English classes were organized around a system of writing folders in which the students kept all their work. These folders were stored in cardboard boxes located on a table at the front of the classroom, and the students picked them up each day as they entered. A couple of times a week, Anna looked at them in order to see what the students had been working on, often writing brief responses on Post-It notes. Describing this practice, one student commented, "She always has a note to leave for each one of us. It's always something—always. I mean she leaves little things like, 'Oh, very good, you should finish writing this piece,' or 'You should have made it just a little bit longer,' or 'You should have described more.'"

Rather than having students work on small daily assignments, such as worksheets, comprehension questions, or grammar exercises as she had done in the past, Anna often engaged her students in projects that lasted for several days or even weeks. For instance, one project that occurred early in the year involved a short story entitled "The Stone Boy" by Gina Berriault. It was about a boy who accidentally killed his brother and then had to deal with his family which would not discuss it. To prepare her students for this story, Anna first had them work in small groups to answer the following question: How do family members react to a death in the family? Then, she asked them to make a list of words that described an appropriate response to death. At Anna's suggestion, I joined one of these groups. It consisted of three girls. After discussing the first question, with one of the students serving as the recorder, we moved on to the list of words.

Sitting with the students gave me a unique perspective on the class. Instead of being an outside observer, I could see the class from *their* point of view. From this perspective, Anna was very much in the periphery; the students were focused more on each other than on her. In fact, when I was sitting with the students, it was easy to lose track of exactly where Anna was in the classroom and what she was doing.

After everyone had completed the pre-reading exercise, Anna directed the group facilitators to distribute the textbooks to their groups, and they began to read orally. However, rather than directing this process by calling on specific students and telling them when to start and stop reading in the traditional round-robin fashion, Anna allowed them to orchestrate the process entirely by themselves. I had never seen anything quite like this. Although she stood at the front of the room, she never said a word. Instead, each reader took the initiative to read a paragraph or two before someone else spontaneously took over. It was a seamless event controlled entirely by the students, who seemed to know exactly what to do. After reading the first page and a half of the story in this fashion, Anna told the students to read the rest of it to themselves. The room then became very quiet as they engrossed themselves in the story. This gave Anna and me an opportunity to talk. Seated across from me at the table next to her desk, she said that after finishing the story and seeing the movie version of the story, they would do a writing assignment in which they would discuss the main character, Arnold, from the point of view of a teacher or a psychologist. She wanted them to write about Arnold's problem and his prognosis from this perspective.

The next time I visited Anna's classroom, the students had already seen the movie and were in the midst of working on their papers. Anna said they had really gotten into this assignment. They had written their first drafts the day before, and one person from each group had gone to the library to look for some psychological terms to describe Arnold. Now, they were reporting back to the class by listing these terms on the board. The terms included words such as neurotic, bizarre remission, contact comfort, kinesics, and simple schizophrenia. When they were finished, Anna asked them to explain what each word meant. This activity occupied the entire class period, and over the next several days, the students wrote several drafts of their papers and received feedback from their classmates along the way. The entire project lasted approximately two weeks.

As the year progressed, Anna's classroom gradually became less teacher-directed, and her instructions for assignments became less specific. She explained that she was much more interested in what a student did with an assignment—how they appropriated it to meet their particular needs—than in how well they followed her particular instructions. In fact, some of their projects did not even emerge from anything that Anna had initiated at all. For instance, one day I arrived at her classroom to find that several of her students were preparing to put on a play based upon Mark Twain's *A Connecticut Yankee in King Arthur's Court.* All of the desks had been moved back to provide room for the performance, and Anna had brought in two boxes of donuts for the students to eat afterwards. I asked Anna how this idea had come about, and she said that one of the students had simply found the play in an old *Scholastic Magazine* in the back of the room and had asked Anna if he and his friends could act it out for extra credit. She said that she had told him, "Sure, as long as you take the responsibility for organizing it." This student and his friends had then planned and orchestrated the entire project without any help or input from Anna. Their performance was impressive. The students were great actors—altering their speech and mannerisms to fit their characters—and the rest of the class was a rapt audience. Afterwards, everyone sat around the room eating the donuts and talking about the play.

The kind of work that students undertook in Anna's classroom was usually open to negotiation—on both a class and an individual basis. Although she often provided some general guidance, Anna allowed the students to adapt her assignments to meet their specific interests and needs as readers and writers and as people. "I try to invite the students to set the agenda," she said.

> A new group of students will be very suspicious—until they see that I'm serious. When they pose agenda items or assignments, I use their language and type up their responses as a group, and we talk about what the possibilities are, what's realistic for us to try to do together, what's important for us to think about together. So, from the beginning, they have a sense that this is not my classroom, but it's our classroom. Ultimately, all of my planning comes out of the things that the students have written about, talked about, requested, and read.

Sometimes, Anna did take a more active role in structuring assignments. Once, in an attempt to introduce the research process to a group of students as a precursor to their senior research papers, she instructed them to pick an unfamiliar city and write a short story that included at least three specific details about this setting. "My goal," she stated, "was to integrate reading and writing in some meaningful way."

> It was a part of the senior curriculum, but I thought beyond that, it would be a useful way for students to extend what they already knew about a topic with the use of the library and their class discussions by collecting information and then incorporating it into something else.

On this occasion, a student who had a personal interest in issues surrounding Black entrepreneurship chose to write a fictional story about what her first day on the job would be like after accepting an upper-level management position in a Houston-based oil company. This task, which required her to do research on both the oil industry and the city of Houston, served to reduce her anxiety toward the larger requirement to write a research paper, and it provided her with a way to use print resources to extend a more familiar form of writing. It was, in essence, a much less daunting task that allowed her to make judgments about the value of research, extend her existing knowledge, and relate it to her personal interests and goals.

Throughout the year, Anna regularly conducted conferences with students in order to discuss works-in-progress. These conferences were sometimes requested by students and other times by Anna. Some of them were one-on-one, while others involved several students at once. Anna said:

> Conferencing has been so vital to my coming to know students. I don't think there is any better way than in the kind of conversation we're having to get to know someone. Students relish that time. They appreciate the opportunity to speak and to be listened to. And typically, the conferences begin with a very general question such as "How are things going?" or "What can I help you with?" And then the student talks and I take notes.

Anna's students agreed that these conferences were an important part of their class. When I asked one of them to describe the strengths of the class, she replied, "It is the open discussion. You get to discuss anything openly—also the writing, the reading, and the conferences with our teacher, the way she will walk us through something if we don't understand."

In addition to these conferences, Anna utilized a system of portfolios for assessment. At the end of each semester, the students went through their work folders and picked out specific pieces of work according to criteria such as their best pieces, their worst pieces, their most important pieces, and their favorite pieces—each accompanied by a one- or two-page essay describing why it was selected. Then, instead of a final exam, the students responded to a series of questions that asked them to reflect on how they had grown as readers and writers throughout the year. These questions included the following: "What have you learned to do best as a writer? Be specific in your response by referring to particular pieces of writing from your folder that you think illustrate your strengths," and "As you search through your folder, look for pieces that help you discuss your own style of writing and those ideas that you think are most important to you."

Although Anna highly valued exercises in self-reflection—not only as a way to inform her practice but also as a way to facilitate student learning—not all of her students saw their merit. Longing for more traditional tests and quizzes, one student said, "I think sometimes you've got to take tests, and hers are so easy. When I looked at the final exam, I said, 'Is this really the final?' I couldn't believe it!" Similarly, another student remarked, "When she told us this was the final exam, I just laughed because it was so easy." These kinds of reactions were typical among students who were attempting to reconcile the difference between their past school experiences in English classrooms and what they were now experiencing with Anna. Invariably, those students who had had Anna as their teacher in the past, and were more familiar with her methods, more fully understood the value in these kinds of exams.

Throughout the year, Anna was not bound by the official curriculum. She seldom followed the official reading list, which consisted of four novels for each grade level that were chosen by the district school board. "I pick and choose," she said. "Of course, our English Department doesn't always have the book that I want. A lot of it depends on what is available. You want to do it and so does everyone else." When I asked her whether or not she ever felt pressure to be more faithful to the list, she replied, "Nobody knows what goes on in here." She admitted that she probably would have been much more nervous about this issue earlier in her career. "I used to follow the textbook," she explained, "until I hit myself in the head with it one day and said, 'Why do we never get out of Puritan America—the 1600s?' We'd spend the entire year on it!"

One time, Anna and I had a lengthy discussion about the textbook. Seated at a table near her desk, we spoke amidst student voices, with the clicking sound of computer keys and the intermittent hum of a dot matrix printer filling the background. "I'll tell you when I really abandoned that book," Anna said. "It was the year when I did an assignment where we looked at the book and asked, 'Who's not in this book?' This was probably my proudest moment in terms of figuring things out. The kids did a whole unit on who wasn't represented in the book. Everybody found somebody who wasn't represented who should have been. Then, we made our own timeline; we wrote historical fiction; we did diaries; and we did point-of-view with characters. We even had a Christmas party where they came as different authors who weren't in the book. After that I gave up the book."

"Then you culminated it all with a giant book-burning in the parking lot," I joked.

"It would have been appropriate," she said.

At this moment, a female student walked past our table on her way to the pencil sharpener, and Anna asked her to get one of the eleventh grade literature textbooks for us to look at. "The literature book— the gold book," Anna explained, while the student stared blankly at the shelf, obviously not knowing which book to grab.

"That's interesting," I remarked. "You have to explain which one it is."

"Oh, I'm sure she's used it before," Anna said. The student finally found the book and brought it to our table.

"How much of this book did you do last year?" Anna asked her. The girl held up her thumb and index finger, indicating about a half-inch.

"That much," Anna commented. "Did you do this stuff at the beginning?" Anna opened the book and pointed to the section on Puritan America.

"No, all we did was a couple of— I don't even remember. It was only like a couple of stories out of here. Most of the time, we did Shakespeare and *Romeo and Juliet.*"

"Did you like the stories that you did out of this book?" I asked.

"I don't know," she said with a slight shrug of her shoulders. "I was asleep." Anna and I both laughed.

"Well, that answers that question," I said.

Flipping through the book and seeing one of the early pages densely packed with obscure Puritan poetry, Anna remarked, "See, I had kids memorizing stuff like this. I can't believe I did that. I'll bet I never got past the double digits. I bet we never got to page 100."

In evaluating her students' work, Anna relied extensively upon the students' own self-assessments. She stated:

> Early in my career, it was really easy for me to just add up all the numbers in the book and divide by whatever number there was accumulated there and write the report card and look at the results. That's become much less easy as I have gone through this transformation, where now I'm eagerly awaiting report cards and for the students to tell me precisely how they've done.

The standards for this evaluation were usually collaboratively negotiated in Anna's classroom. As the students proceeded through the writing process, they were encouraged to share their works-in-progress with their peers—either in small groups or with the whole class—and it was through the resulting dialogue that the characteristics of good writing were identified. Anna also participated in this process, but she was careful not to dominate the discussion. When students read each other's papers in these informal writing groups, the qualities that they defined as the strengths of particular pieces became their measures of success. In this way, the class defined their own standards.

The actual assigning of grades in Anna's classroom usually took place through student/teacher conferences, which occurred after particular pieces of writing were completed. One of her students explained the process as follows:

> We read the paper and we'll talk about it. Then, we'll have little groups, and we'll go up to Ms. Henson and talk to her about our grades. She'll give us her opinion about the paper, and we'll give her our opinion, and we'll talk about it. She'll say, "Well, I come up with the grade such-and-such," and you'll say, "Well, I think I should get such-and-such." You talk about that and you accommodate each other.

In these conferences, Anna typically invited the students to discuss what grade they felt best reflected the work they had done on a specific piece and why, and this grade was then entered in the official grade book— often by the students themselves. "I think grades sort of belong to the students," she said, "and grade books should be there for them to observe. In fact, when they complete assignments they actually check them off in the grade book themselves. It's always there and it's always open." Very much aware of how an over-emphasis on grades can undermine students' intrinsic motivation to write and take their work seriously, Anna tried to defer the actual assignment of grades as long as possible. "It has really helped put the emphasis on the intrinsic value of the work, rather than working for a grade, which has no currency, no value at all, outside of school or anywhere, really."

None of Anna's students with whom I interacted were critical of her grading policy. They thought it was an exceedingly fair process. "I think it's fair—real fair," a student told me. Continuing, he stated:

> It is fair because you have one-on-one contact with your teacher. It's not like you know you did *A* work, but you look at your report card and all of the sudden, you have *B-* and you want to know why. Most teachers don't want to explain why they came up with a particular grade. With Ms. Henson, you sit down and you calculate, and she's calculating too, and you compare. And if she comes up with something that you didn't come up with, you can talk it out and reason with her, and back it up with your folder.

In addition to formal grades, Anna also utilized a system of check-marks to document each student's progress, thus enabling her to keep close tabs on how many pieces students were working on, how many they had completed, how group projects were progressing, and what their attendance patterns were like. To Anna, this kind of information was far more useful in describing students' achievements than a mere list of grades. "In my classroom," she said, "a grade is almost an irrelevant thing."

The timing for the completion of writing tasks was relatively open-ended, with the students setting their own pace for individual pieces of writing in their folders. Anna tried to prevent elements of the school context, such as marking period dates, to constrain the students' decision-making in this area. Deadlines were loosely set, with Anna acknowledging that some students needed an announced due date to help them work toward task-completion, but changes in the due date were always negotiable. "I used to be much more traditional in the sense that I expected all papers to be finished at a certain time," she said. "But now, the deadline is when the piece is finished, and that call is made by the student, perhaps in collaboration with other writers and other readers." Some students responded well to this kind of structure, while others complained that Anna was too easy on them. One student told me:

> I think Ms. Henson is too lenient. Now, don't get me wrong. It's kind of good, but I mean, half of the people in here don't even have their work done. Half of the people that you ask about their poetry books may only have one poem. I don't want her to be too hard, where she's just on us continuously, but sometimes I wish Ms. Henson would say, "Do this now," instead of just saying, "Well, you've gotta have that in. Don't forget."

Nevertheless, Anna was thoroughly convinced that her students were more productive in her current classroom than they had ever been when it was more traditional. The evidence was in their folders—even if not all of the students appreciated it.

Another characteristic of Anna's classroom was a free-flow of talk. Virtually every time I visited, the students were sitting in groups, doing their work, and talking freely. Some were talking about their papers, while others were talking about non-school-related things. Anna never attempted to regulate the kind of talk that her students did. She never told students to stop having a particular conversation. However, she did ask the students to lower their voices when the noise level got too loud, and she often allowed students to go to the library when they needed a more quiet place to work. Few of Anna's students had ever been afforded this kind of freedom in their other classes, yet they clearly recognized its benefit. In explaining how talk influenced his work, one male student told me:

> By talking to each other, by sharing our thoughts with one another, and congregating with one another, we get more ideas about what we want to put in our paper, how we want to start our paper off, how we want to end our paper, or what words or what kinds of vocabulary should we use, or should we change our paper.

Another student said:

> Well, people are going to talk regardless. If you go to a class,
> and it's like, "No talking, just sit there and do your work,"
> it's not fun. You have to learn in a comfortable environment.
> I guess that's what she's trying to set. You work at your own
> pace, and talk to your friends, conversate and stuff. But some-
> times when you talk to your friends or what-not, that sparks
> your creative writing....

Whenever I asked Anna's students about the usefulness of talking in
their classroom, they virtually always gave these kinds of responses—
and when I shared this information with Anna, she remarked, "That's
affirming to me, to read that students know that the talk is intentional,
that there is reason that it's allowed, that it's not just avoiding something
else. They know that it can be purposeful."

As the year progressed, all of Anna's classes developed a strong sense
of community. The students seemed to genuinely care about themselves
and each other, and how the entire class was progressing. Conflicts were
exceedingly rare. Some students even intentionally missed other classes
so they could remain in Anna's room and continue to work. It was obvious that she cared very deeply about them as students and as people, and
they reciprocated. In describing what she liked best about Anna's classroom, one female student stated quite eloquently:

> I think that Ms. Henson is about the only teacher that I have
> had at Windrow, besides Ms. Mosenthal, that ever really cared,
> who talked to me and asked me how I was doing.... She's
> concerned, and that makes me more concerned. It's a snow-
> ball reaction. Somebody has to care, and I care the utmost.
> With her caring too, you're working as one, and we get more
> accomplished that way. If she didn't care, then that would
> make me have a different feel about the class. It would be a
> whole other ballgame.

Anna's Underlying Beliefs

In the sub-sections that follow, I describe the underlying beliefs that guided Anna's teaching practices. Through my analysis of in-

terview transcripts and other documents, I identified three categories of beliefs: 1) her beliefs about literacy; 2) her beliefs about teaching; and 3) her beliefs about students.[20] It is important to understand that these categories were entirely my creation, not Anna's. Throughout our many interviews and informal conversations, Anna never overtly labeled or compartmentalized her thinking in this way. Thus, these categories should be viewed solely as a rhetorical strategy for organizing and presenting my analyses, and not as a literal representation of how Anna herself constructed her beliefs.

Beliefs about Literacy

Most of Anna's beliefs about literacy stemmed from her personal life experiences, and from her career-long observations of children and how they learn—rather than directly from formal theories of literacy.[21] Early in her career, she was somewhat influenced by the perspectives that were put forth in her college courses and which were also expounded in the research literature of the day, but many of these beliefs proved to be short-lived. She discarded them rather quickly after trying to put them into practice and not being satisfied with the results. For example, as a beginning teacher, she readily accepted the notion that literacy was synonymous with the mastery of skills. At that time, in late 1960s and early 1970s, mastery learning and skills-based instruction were the dominant approaches to teaching reading, and she felt obliged to use them in her classroom. Anna said, "There was this notion that if you could master syllables, then you'd understand words; and once you knew words, you'd know sentences; and once you knew sentences, you'd build paragraphs. But real reading doesn't occur that way, and writing doesn't either."

When Anna was a preservice teacher and throughout much of her later career, the standard view of literacy focused solely on reading, with writing being almost totally ignored. "Writing was something that everyone assumed you could either do or you couldn't do," she explained.

> It wasn't a question of learning how to do it better. You either had the talent for it or you didn't. We know so much more now about how students acquire writing and how they build writing skills, but that was something that my methods classes didn't prepare me for at all. We concentrated on reading, exclusively.

When Anna did have her students write in those initial years, her approach tended to be methodical and formulaic. "Early on," she said, "my expectations were very traditional. Everybody needed to know how to write a business letter, how to distinguish a personal letter from a business letter—the textbook approach to genre." The entire emphasis was on the mastery of form; the content and the purpose of the writing were virtually irrelevant.

In contrast, as an experienced teacher Anna believed in the importance of emphasizing the utilitarian value of literacy. "When students have something to say and a reason to communicate," she said, "they can write very efficiently and effectively." Anna knew from her own life experiences—from her parents and her grandparents—that reading and writing were practical tools for communication, not ends unto themselves. However, she did not initially draw a connection between this knowledge and her classroom practices. Anna explained:

> At first, I wasn't paying attention to any of the things that students were trying to communicate. That wasn't even important to the lesson. The worksheets—if you got the *-ing* in the right place, or if you put the *-ed* where it was supposed to go, if you understood the singular or past tense, plurals with no *s*, then you knew how to do things. That's what was important. Forget that you might have a really compelling story to tell. Forget that there was anything important to say.

In the real world of Anna's parents and grandparents, reading and writing were important because they served useful roles in their lives. The letters that her mother read and composed brought the family together and enabled them to imagine the lives of those who remained in the "Old Country." Although Anna knew the power of stories in her own life, she did not initially value them as a teaching tool—which is not surprising, given the emphasis of her college courses. "All through my college education," she said, "story-telling and narrative weren't valued very highly."

> We weren't taught any ways of using children's own lives, for example, in an English curriculum. It was always how to present some canonical piece, all the books that had been prescribed over the years that were deemed important. That's what we needed to know. So, when I left college, that's virtually all I knew, except for my own stories.

One of Anna's most fundamental beliefs about literacy—one which greatly influenced what she did in her classroom during my visits—was the idea that reading and writing were an important means for self-discovery. In one of our interviews, she remarked, "I think that deciding who we are and what we think is pretty important.... Kids should be encouraged to grow in their own direction and learn who they are. The time we spend talking, reading, and writing should be guided by that notion." Anna held this belief throughout much of her life. In 1975, she wrote a paper for a college course that expressed the same sentiment. "In terms of philosophy," she wrote, "my ultimate concern is knowing oneself. Writing allows an individual a maximum awareness of his own being in relationship to other individuals and experiences." However, this belief was generally unsupported by her experiences as a preservice teacher.

Closely related to Anna's perception of literacy as a tool for self-reflection was the idea that students should be encouraged to choose their own topics and evaluate their own work. Regarding the issue of topic choice, she explained:

> I'm more and more strongly convinced that the students have to generate their own ideas. That business of assigned topics is sort of a power play on the part of teachers to maintain control over the writing process. I think there are ways to explore things that students may know about without my being the presenter of those ideas and those forms.

Anna said that she always felt this way—even as a young teacher. "Early on," she explained, "I probably always felt that students should choose their own topics. I don't remember it being an issue or a problem. Having to think up things to write about is such an integral part of being a writer." Anna was long guided by the notion that writing in school should be modeled after writing in the "real world," and this idea influenced her feeling about the importance of self-evaluation. She said, "Again, it's modeled on real world writing, where the first person who judges what you are saying is you. You are always the first reader of your writing."

In summary Anna's beliefs about literacy fell into two main subcategories. On the one hand, there were transitory beliefs that arose primarily through her university experiences as a preservice teacher—while on the other hand, there were longstanding and enduring beliefs that were deeply rooted in her personal life experiences. And, when these two kinds of beliefs clashed, it was usually the latter which prevailed.

Beliefs about Teaching

Anna's beliefs about teaching also emerged from her life-long experiences—both as a student and as a teacher. Throughout our conversations, she frequently referred to past incidents in order to explain why she held a particular idea or belief. For example, one belief that she held about her role as a teacher could best be summarized through the dictum, "Do no harm." She said, "You know, doctors have their rule, 'Do no harm.' I think if we have one fundamental rule in teaching, it should be a rule like that." To Anna, harm could take many forms. It could be a vindictive teacher who uses grades to punish a student for non-conformity, or it could be a well-meaning teacher who inadvertently impedes a student while trying to help. In relating this belief to a specific past experience, she said:

> I think that's one of my night school revelations. I saw where I had done harm, where I had been instrumental in keeping someone from becoming who they needed to be. And I just wasn't alert enough, aware enough, in tune enough, to see that.

Citing another personal incident, she explained how she had unwittingly caused students discomfort by praising them in front of their peers.

> I'm sensitive to our younger males who hang in the back of the room and are dying to say the answers, but I just can't put them in the situation where they violate peer codes. I've really learned that over the years, especially from a couple of students who took me aside and said, "Please don't do that to me." And I had to apologize and know that I was doing something that a teacher should know better than to do. I'm much more careful about that now—about providing the whole class with a situation where "student X" is going to be known by everyone as the only person who read the story last night.

Another belief that Anna held about her role as a teacher involved the inappropriateness of "preaching" to students. In explaining what she meant by this term, she said:

> [Preaching] is when people say what everybody else has to do to be successful, as if the whole world judges everyone by a well-defined set of standards. It is almost a businessman's approach to teaching English—the expressing of values that represent only a very small segment of social interaction. In the real world, as I look around, I see successful people of all class and all color who define acceptable standards in very different and much broader ways. I have just never felt comfortable trying to define or say those kinds of things to a whole class of students.

Anna traced this reluctance, at least in part, to her own experiences as a student. She said that she could remember sitting in school and being "bored to death" when teachers were preaching to her. "They were history teachers," she said, "and they were preaching."

> And I was going to have to go home that night and try to explain what we did in history, and my parents were not going to want to hear what this nun had said all day…. It clearly was not history.

In addition, Anna felt that her reluctance could also have been a function of her personality. "You know, if I get a good idea, I may ask someone to help me think it through, but I'm not one who can easily say, 'I know what you should be doing.'" Smiling, she continued, "Half the time, I'm not sure I know what I'm supposed to be doing, so please don't get me trying to tell somebody else what to do."

For Anna, having a willingness to learn was an important part of being a teacher. The fact that she continually took college courses throughout her career—even when they were not required and there was no significant salary incentive—illustrated the strength of her commitment to formal learning. However, she also valued the informal ideas and insights that she gained from listening to and learning from her students and her colleagues. Anna's story about how she learned the importance of creating a classroom community in her first year at Windrow, her decision to teach students in night school in order to better understand why they had failed her class during the day, and her grading conference with Jackie all exemplified some of the ways that she learned from her students. She also learned from other teachers. In describing her relationship with her colleagues, she said:

> I am not a teacher who extends stuff much beyond my own classroom. I have conversations and encourage other teachers to think about things if they're open and willing. But I'm not one who walks into someone's room and says, 'You gotta try this.' I'm not a proselytizer.... Instead, I have tried to learn from colleagues because I know that they've done good things that have been really successful with students.

Anna was always keenly aware of the limits of her job, believing that it was not appropriate for a teacher to try to "save" children. In one of our conversations, I once remarked, "I've seen some teachers who become like surrogate mothers to their students, who want to adopt kids or take them home as foster children, but I don't see any of that in you." Her response provided an insight into her thinking. She said:

> To tell you the truth, I think those are dangerous attitudes for teachers to have, and I've always guarded against it. It presupposes a relationship with students that we just don't have, given the numbers of students we have to work with. To try to "rescue" students is unfair because you can't do it with everyone. It's simply not a way that I've ever constructed being a teacher.... I'm not a person who pries into the private lives of children. I think that they're entitled to privacy and that the school is a place where they can get away. It's none of my business if a student doesn't want to talk about themself, and I don't have any business asking.

In an interview conducted by another researcher, Anna reiterated this sentiment. Reflecting on her early days of teaching, she said, "I didn't want to be a teacher who was going to go into the classroom and save anybody. I was interested in literature. I knew the excitement of books. I could share *that*."

Although Anna was not comfortable in forming "motherly" relationships with her students, she did believe that she had a duty to respond to their individual needs. "One of the difficult things about teaching is balancing the needs of the individual against the needs of the group," she said. "And that's something I've grown to recognize as part of my role as teacher—how to satisfy that tenuous balance." Anna preferred to have a student-centered classroom in which the students assumed a high degree of responsibility for how the class ran, but she was careful not to foist this approach upon groups that were unready or unwilling to accept it. For example, during one of my early visits to her classroom, I saw her do a lesson with a group of ninth-grade remedial students that was much more teacher-directed than anything that I ever saw her do with her older students. Afterwards, she explained the difference as follows:

> It's been a difficult task for me. I understand what they're looking for. We've had a lot of talks in the classroom about "Why aren't you willing take this responsibility for yourselves?" And there are a few kids in the class who are self-motivated and who, in fact, go to the library. They ask to be permitted out of the class because they don't like the teacherly presentational mode. But the majority of that class have asked for it. They say, "We want you to tell us how to do things." I have an obligation to respond to my students, and I'm willing to do it.

Nevertheless, Anna believed that it was important for teachers to challenge students, and she was not adverse to making them feel uncomfortable in a given situation—as long as it urged them to think or it facilitated their growth in some way. "*That*, I feel obliged to do," she said, "but in an atmosphere where making a mistake and failing is an acceptable thing to do, another step toward learning." Anna felt that students learned through failure—not failure in the form of a letter grade assigned by a teacher, but failure in the form of taking risks, not succeeding, and continuing to try. "Kids need to develop a sense of trust in a teacher's willingness to help them through a problem paper," she explained.

> And I have to be careful not to be immediately judgmental and throw up my hands and say, "Just because you didn't do it right the first time, it's not good." I do have that core of teacherly stuff in me that reacts, and I have to watch those reactions because kids are sensitive.

Throughout our conversations, Anna sometimes referred to past beliefs about teaching that she no longer held. For example, she said that she used to feel it was important to maintain a quiet and orderly classroom with student socializing kept at a minimum. "I used to think that the model classroom was the room where the teacher was doing the talking and that all the students were attentively listening," she said. "That was my personal model of learning and the way I had been schooled.... I thought my number one job was to intervene in all socializing and keep it to a minimum." Anna also felt pressure from her colleagues to keep an orderly classroom. She feared that she would be considered a bad teacher if she did not meet this basic expectation. At the same time, she was aware of the role that socializing had played in her own life as a student. "I was the only female with three male siblings, and school was the place where I would meet friends," she explained. "I mean it had to be a social place for me, but I think I forgot that when I started teaching." In explaining how her thinking gradually evolved, she said:

> I can't say that it was a single experience. It was really a series of experiences. Part of it had to do with incorporating student-teachers into the classroom. The student-teacher and I would have dialogues—we would be talking—and we could see that our conversations weren't interfering with student work. So why would student conversations interfere with student work? It all sounds so fundamentally simple, but it took me a long time to realize that. Talking is important for adults. We can sit in church and movies and faculty meetings and do side-conversations with friends, and it doesn't detract from what's going on. Everybody leaves knowing exactly what they need to know. Yet, when kids do that in class, we somehow view it as being disruptive, and we over-react, and the focus of the class becomes distorted. Then, Johnny, who has something really important to say, becomes the center of all the wrong kinds of attention....

When she first began to teach, Anna also believed that it was her job to identify and correct all of her students' errors. That was the way she defined her job. "I saw myself very traditionally as the person who was to mitigate error. My job was to stand between the students' texts and the ideal writing." Anna explained that this conception of teaching was short-lived and relatively easy to give up. "I'd be so charmed by a piece of writing that I would just stop and say, 'Look, this is too effective to be destroyed by me.'" Searching for other ways to respond to student texts, she turned to the students themselves and began encouraging them to write about their own writing.

> I've found those pieces of [reflective] writing so perceptive. It's useful to me as a teacher when students can define where they're having problems in places that I often would not recognize as a reader. In places where I would be stymied by a traditional error, students recognize that it's not terribly important and that things can be worked on later.

Another belief that Anna held early in her career was the idea that the teacher was the sole audience for student work. Although she always had visitors coming into her classroom—such as poets and other writers who shared their work with students—it never occurred to her to have students read and critique each other's writing. She also did not involve their parents. "I felt that it was my responsibility to comment on student writing," she said, "and that to ask that of a parent was somehow shifting the burden." Over the years, however, Anna gradually saw the value of extending the notion of audience beyond the teacher, and beyond the classroom. She said:

> Now, I encourage kids to show their work to everybody. I'm one reader. I'm not the only reader. It's really important to me that students have a bigger sense of the importance of what they do. If they're only doing it for me, there's no point in doing it at all. And that's really a message I'm trying to communicate now, and have for the last few years. "If the only reason you're writing this paper is for a grade from Ms. Henson, then you're wasting your time."

Finally, as a beginning teacher, Anna believed that the curriculum was a fixed and immutable document and that it was her job to "present" it to the students. In her mind, there was no room for negotiation. "When I first started teaching," she said, "I thought the curriculum was like a bible, and I really looked for that kind of guidance." But the assistance that Anna craved was not immediately forthcoming. During her first few years of teaching at Franklin Junior High, the curriculum was always a fuzzy concept that remained just beyond her grasp. In fact, she had a very difficult time even obtaining a written copy of it. She explained:

> I didn't know what the junior high curriculum for English was. Nothing was ever given to me with the explanation that here were the requirements that should be met by the end of the semester—or that my students were here and this was where they needed to go.

Without knowing the official curriculum, Anna said that she simply "winged it"—using the textbooks that were given to her and thinking, "This must be the curriculum." She said that she did not realize that other schools used other books. It was only after several years of teaching that she finally discovered that the school district did indeed possess explicit objectives for reading and writing. But instead of helping her, they constrained her. To Anna, the curriculum seemed like something so fixed and so permanent that there was no room for a teacher to make adjustments. "As a young teacher, I just didn't think I had a right to fool around with those pieces of information that the school board shared with us," she said. But after seeing how the system actually worked, she gradually began to feel empowered to make appropriate changes. "[Curriculum mandates] came in funny ways," she remarked, "and they disappeared just as oddly."

> No one said, "Withdraw or throw out those pages. We're no longer doing that." Their usefulness would just sort of run out. The steam behind a curriculum push would exhaust itself.... Back in the late '70s and early '80s I started to feel more autonomous as a teacher and feel that I didn't have to honor the givens as much as I did early on. And I eventually felt that I didn't even have to pay attention to those any more. I understood my responsibility in a more holistic way. I knew that I was teaching reading and writing—the fundamental speaking and listening—but felt that I could do it in the most efficient way possible. Ultimately, the students were much more central to my understanding of how to do that than any guidebook.

In summary, Anna's beliefs about teaching fell into two basic subcategories: past and present. While her past beliefs were largely shaped by her own childhood experiences in school, her present beliefs gradually evolved over time in response to the specific contexts in which her teaching career was situated. As a teacher, Anna continually reflected upon and reformed her prior thinking about teaching—readily modifying those ideas and expectations that proved to be dysfunctional when she tried to put them into practice. At the same time, she more fully embraced those beliefs that seemed to work, so that her entire belief system, while continually changing and evolving, was remarkably stable over time.

Beliefs about Students

Anna's beliefs about students were closely related to her attitude toward people in general. Anna felt strongly that everyone had inherent worth and dignity, and she treated them accordingly—without exception. One of the first things that I noticed in visiting her classroom was the respectful way in which she interacted with her students; she treated them the same way she would treat another adult. To Anna, mutual respect was a crucial part of any teacher/student relationship. "I've argued with other teachers about this," she said, "but I think that with students respect has to be an unconditional thing. I am employed by them. I owe them respect." Early in her career, however, she probably would not have voiced this sentiment. Instead, she would have said that teachers were owed respect while students had to earn it. That was the way most of her colleagues felt. It was the underlying assumption that pervaded her work environment—an assumption that she had accepted without question. "But that's not how I see things now," she explained.

> When we think about humanity, and if we want to really teach the value of respect and why that's an important value for communication, then we have to be unconditional in our willingness to show respect to students, no matter what we see. If we want students to listen to us, no matter how offensive we can be, we have to be willing to listen when students are offensive too. I think students sense that and understand that profoundly without any explanation.

Anna also possessed a strong faith in her students' ability to assume responsibility for themselves and to make good decisions about things that ultimately affect their lives—things such as education. "Children have much more ability, good sense, intellectual integrity, and commitment to school than we ever give them credit for," she exclaimed. Anna had held this belief for a long time—perhaps for her entire career. In only her fourth year as a teacher, while still teaching at Franklin Junior High School, she wrote in a paper for a college course:

> Every student is a human being and using that tired analogy of the acorn shares the potential for greatness. Helping young people discover themselves, their ideas, and their aspirations with a concern for their potential and ability to act out that potential; to establish powers of thought and develop the ability to reason and choose freely what is right are ambitious goals for a teacher but goals that should not be undermined.

Thus, even as a beginning teacher struggling to be successful, Anna expressed an optimistic view of her students with an unyielding faith in their potential as human beings, and this belief remained fairly constant throughout her entire career. It was her teaching practices that gradually changed. Anna explained:

> By the time students get to my room, they've been in school ten years. They know what's expected, and they start tinkering and retooling, and they help me see the wonderful things that kids can do in creating their own curriculum. I don't have to be the center of it. There are times that I don't even have to be a part of it. There's no mistaking that I am their teacher, however. Students understand that, but they also understand that they have a more powerful role than maybe they've ever experienced before in designing the work that they want to undertake. And they are willing to do so much more than the puny things that I used to ask of them. I'm embarrassed to think of some of the assignments I've given over the years.

Anna viewed her students as more than just consumers of literature; she viewed them as people too. "A child does not have to excel in reading and writing in order to play an important role in my classroom," she explained. Instead, she tried to embrace all students equally. Anna attributed this attitude to her childhood experience of growing up with immigrant grandparents who were not literate in English. "My home experience taught me that people who didn't go to school could be good people and were good people," she said, "and that it wasn't schooling alone that made someone valuable." But it was many years before she began to operationalize this belief in her classroom practices. Initially, she based much of her teaching upon the much more commonly expressed idea that students were simply lacking in skills.

> In the early years, I thought of the students in a deficit mode, that they were coming without skills, coming without ways of doing the work they needed to do. Every time I've been able to give up the notion of what they can't do, I've recognized along with them a multitude of things that they can do. It makes so much more sense to build on what they already know and to extend what they already know.

Anna believed in a student-centered approach in the truest sense of the term. She felt that students should play a significant role in determining how they spend their time in her classroom. She said:

> I can't set a purpose for the student to do the work, because I can't be the internal motivation. It can't be limited to the school, to the textbooks, or doing my assignments. Nobody is going to grow intellectually or emotionally or socially from responding to some arbitrary task that I set for them. Just assuming that makes me laugh. That's a ridiculous proposition.

This idea stemmed both from her natural discomfort in assuming an authoritarian role and from her own observations about how students learn. "There are only a couple of things that we control, really," she said.

> Teachers believe that they have control over what kids are thinking, but we know better. Look at your traditional classroom. If the teacher talks, we don't know what the kids are thinking. Just because they are looking at us doesn't mean they are listening to us or believing us or understanding what we're saying.

Therefore, Anna tried to provide her students with genuine opportunities for determining the kinds of work that they undertook, as well as authentic responsibility for establishing the daily rhythm and flow of the class-room. For example, during one of our early interviews, I remarked that there never seemed to be a definite point at which her classes officially began. Instead, the students almost always began to work on their own without any overt cues from Anna. In reply, Anna said:

> I'm pleased that's your perception because I've consciously worked toward students being responsible for the momentum and the flow from the class. Students assume that kind of responsibility for themselves when they know that the issues they're raising are the issues that are going to concern us, and I'm not the person who's going to get us started—nor will I be the person who stops, interferes, or disrupts. If we really believe that it is important for kids to have authority and for kids to take responsibility for their learning, then we have to allow them these kinds of opportunities.

Talking also played an important role in Anna's classroom. Early in her career, when she thought it was the teacher's job to talk and the students' job to listen, she viewed student-talking as a subversive activity—something that the teacher had to strictly control. As an experienced teacher, however, Anna felt that talking was an important way that students learned. "When teachers talk about speech, they think oratory," she said, "and I've been convincing myself that speech really means just talking and having a conversation. Students seldom have an opportunity to value talk as a learning tool." In explaining her rationale for this perspective, she said:

> We know how we learn things. Most of what we've learned is from one another, just from our everyday exchanges. We may read the newspaper for information, but the way in which I really learned how to function in the world of Windrow High School was from listening, and watching, and talking to people—not from reading a manual on how to be a good teacher here. So I feel that we need to give students the same kinds of experience.

Of course, Anna was keenly aware of the difficulty of putting this belief into practice. How did she get her students to share in her view about talking? How did she convey the idea that their talking in class had a higher purpose than mere socializing? How did she convince them that she was not simply abdicating her responsibility to maintain a quiet classroom? Recognizing the importance of these questions, Anna explained:

> A lot of kids have trouble with it, as you can imagine, so I don't start the school year announcing, "This is going to be a different kind of class." I really begin a class with a very traditional look, so that I don't undermine student expectations. They think that this is an English class, a serious one; it's an Honors class, and there are high expectations of them. They know that an English class looks a certain way. The desks will all be in rows, and I'll be very pleasant but stern. We'll write and we'll talk, and we'll move very slowly.

Finally, Anna believed that students had an obligation to learn who they were and what they thought. For her, the development of a sense of self was a very important goal of education. She said, "For all the revisionism that we've seen in curriculum change and reform talk, I've found that every kid really presents the same question: 'Who am I and where do I fit in an increasingly hostile world?'" This was an unarticulated question, of course—one which she admitted her students would probably not feel comfortable discussing directly—but, in Anna's opinion, it was still very important. "Who am I?" Anna saw her students continually posing this question in virtually everything they did; it drove their lives. Therefore, she strove to make it central to her classroom.

Like her beliefs about literacy and her beliefs about teaching, Anna's beliefs about students fell into two basic subcategories. First, there were her past beliefs, which were largely based on her own experiences as a student. These beliefs tended not to withstand her scrutiny, and she either discarded or modified them over time. Second, there were her present beliefs which were deeply rooted in her basic life experiences and which had withstood the test of time. These beliefs were an integral part of her personality—her psyche—the very essence of who she was as a person—and they directly guided the way she interacted with students.

Summary

Anna's contemporary teaching practices were closely related to her underlying beliefs about literacy, teaching and students. However, the relationship was not always a close one. Early in her career, Anna possessed a variety of beliefs that arose from a combination of her childhood experiences in school and her university experiences as a preservice teacher. These transitory, school-based beliefs guided many of her early teaching practices. For example, she initially taught reading as a skill with lots of worksheets, and her writing assignments tended to be teacher-directed and formulaic. At the same time, however, Anna possessed a core of more enduring beliefs that were deeply rooted in her childhood and adult experiences beyond school. For example, remembering her family experiences with her parents and grandparents, she strongly believed that reading and writing were exciting, dynamic activities that had utilitarian functions—but this belief had little initial impact on her early teaching practices. It was not until she tried to implement teaching practices based upon her school-based beliefs, and was dissatisfied with the results, that she gradually began to explore other ways of teaching.

Over time, Anna either abandoned or reshaped many of her prior beliefs and drew upon others to create a functional pedagogy. It was a practical move—one that she made in response to the demands of her job—and the transition was slow, haphazard, and idiosyncratic, with no definite beginning or end. The one thing that remained constant was Anna's desire to be a successful teacher and her commitment to be critically self-reflective about her beliefs and practices.

EPILOGUE

In the preceding chapters, I have told the story of Anna's professional development, contextualized within the story of my own development as a student, a teacher, and a researcher. I began with an extended personal narrative which detailed some of the experiences that have shaped my values and beliefs about teaching, literacy, and research. Then, I reviewed the literature on teacher thinking that informed my survey study in Kentucky and inspired my collaboration with Anna, and I explained why I ultimately abandoned this methodology in favor of a life history approach. Next, I explored some of the epistemological underpinnings of life history research, illustrating my arguments through stories of my encounter with a work of art and my conversation with a former professor. Finally, after situating my work with Anna within the broader context of my own life as a student, a teacher, and a researcher, I told Anna's story. Using life history and ethnographic methods, I chronicled the evolution of Anna's teaching career, with a particular emphasis on her underlying beliefs about literacy, teaching, and students, which helped to shape her teaching practices. In this section, I discuss some of the implications of my work.

Although an in-depth life history study of the beliefs and practices of a single teacher has little value for making generalizations about other teachers in a statistical sense, it can be extremely useful as a vehicle for elaborating an understanding of one's own beliefs and practices. Donmoyer (1990) makes a compelling argument for expanding the notion of generalizability to include the learning that people experience when they read about single cases. As a beginning teacher, I would have greatly valued reading storied accounts of others teachers who had struggled through situations similar to my own, if for no other reason than simply to have known that I was not alone. Teaching is a solitary profession in which practitioners have limited opportunities to interact with their colleagues. When I was a special education teacher in Kentucky, I sometimes went for days, weeks even, without ever having significant interactions with other adults. My classroom was located in the basement of the school, physically isolated from the other classrooms—a convenient, out-of-the-way place for the administration to "warehouse" those students with special needs. Other teachers seldom ventured down to my room, while at the same time, I was not allowed to leave.[22] Within this socially barren existence, reading narrative accounts of other teachers' experiences would have been one way that I could have overcome my feelings of isolation.

Narrative accounts of teachers' lives and careers can also serve as tools for self-reflection. Knowing Anna has enabled me to rethink some of my past experiences from a different perspective—to re-imagine my life as a teacher in light of my new knowledge and experiences, and to reflect on how things might have been different. After visiting Anna's classroom for an extended period and studying her beliefs and practices, I now realize that as a beginning teacher I was far too concerned with following the "correct" procedure—doing the right things, rather than doing the things that were right for me and my students. Through my early family experiences I knew the power of personal stories, yet I largely ignored my students' stories as a vehicle for their learning. I drew instead upon a vast and impersonal body of knowledge that had been systematically mapped out by others and presented to me as prescriptions for my practice. Ultimately, this kind of knowledge was not very useful to me or to my students.

By telling my own story, in addition to Anna's, I hope to provide readers with a tool for reflecting upon *their* lives—*their* beliefs and practices. While I realize that not all readers will identify with my experiences, I believe that my writing can nonetheless serve as a starting point for any teacher who is inclined to be self-reflective. By examining the connections between my story and Anna's story, and actively weighing them against their own ongoing life experiences, readers may gain deeper insights into the underlying beliefs, assumptions, and experiences that shape their own teaching and research practices. Engaging in this kind of self-reflection has been shown to be an important part of teachers' professional growth and development (see, e.g., Cole & Knowles, et al., 2000; Dick, 1993; Ebbs, 1995/1996; Gustafson, 1993/1995; Holt-Reynolds, 1994; Knowles, 1993; Koivu-Rybicki, 1995/1996; Smith, 1994; Tann, 1993; Winikates, 1995/1996).

Transforming my Practice as a Teacher Educator

Knowing Anna has helped me to make a closer connection between my own beliefs and practices as a teacher educator. For several years—both before, during, and after my study with Anna—I have taught reading and writing methods courses for preservice elementary teachers at the University of Michigan and Western Michigan University. At first, my teaching was very traditional. I delivered lectures, led discussions, gave assignments, issued grades, and did all of the other things that college instructors typically do. That was the way I had been taught as a student in college, and that was what I felt my students expected. I worked hard at being a "good" teacher following this approach, and my students were generally appreciative of my efforts. One student wrote in her end-of-the-course evaluation:

> Jim is very enthusiastic and <u>dedicated</u> to his work. He motivates students by showing that he really cares about their progress. We <u>always</u> got our graded assignments back promptly, yet you could tell that he had put time into reading and grading them.... I think he did a <u>great</u> job.

Nevertheless, I felt uncomfortable in the role that I had created for myself. As a shy person, I did not like being the center of attention all of the time. I did not like being the "knowledge-giver" and the sole judge of student success. I did not like assigning letter grades, which always seemed to undermine students' intrinsic motivation and was usually an unspoken source of tension within my classroom. Grading was a powerful force that influenced the kinds of relationships that I was able to have with students. During my office hours, I resented having to continually counsel students about their grades. I wanted them to care about the course content—to discuss *that* during my office hours—not just their grades.

One of my university colleagues once remarked, "Teaching undergraduates is truly a thankless job. You work your butt off trying to get them involved, and all they really care about is their grade." I understood exactly what this colleague meant, although I tried not to be as cynical. Like any high-achieving college students, my students were quick to express a concern whenever they received anything lower than an *A* on an assignment. However, I did not blame them for this pre-occupation. Letter grades are the universal currency in schools, and it was through their careful attention to grades that these students had amassed the "academic capital" necessary to attend college in the first place. I knew that it was unrealistic for me to expect them to suddenly stop playing a game that they had played so successfully for their entire lives. Nevertheless, the problem remained. On the one hand, I felt compelled to assign grades, while, on the other hand, I knew that grades were undermining the teaching and learning in my classroom.

My work with Anna gave me an important insight into dealing with this problem. Having experienced a similar frustration in her own teaching, Anna had responded by letting go of her past, dysfunctional belief about the importance of the teacher being the sole arbiter of a student's work, and embracing her more enduring belief that students should be encouraged to make decisions for themselves. With this shift in her thinking came a shift in her practices, as she gradually began to share authority for assigning grades with her students. By visiting Anna's classroom and observing how she had dealt with this issue, I began to reflect on my own beliefs and practices and developed a more internally-consistent pedagogy. Deep down, I had never been comfortable as an authoritarian-style teacher—yet, throughout my career, I had always assumed an authoritarian stance. Why had I done this? I had done it because that was what I knew. Throughout all of my experiences as a student and all of my experiences as a preservice teacher, I had developed a veneer of beliefs and expectations about teaching that prevented me from seeing or embracing other possibilities.

Inspired by my observations of Anna's teaching, but not copying her practices directly, I decided to address the issue of grades in a way that honored my deeper sense of who I was as a person. Put simply, I told all of my students, in advance, that they would receive *A*s for the course. I realize how naive and idealistic this may sound, but I did not make my decision lightly. Although I never discussed my plan with Anna, I did tell several of my university colleagues, and they strongly advised me not to do it. They warned that the students would certainly take advantage of me and would not do quality work. Nevertheless, I was determined to try. Having already taught this course for several semesters, I felt that I knew how my students would respond. Most of my students in past semesters had earned *A*s or *B*s, so I knew I would probably not be giving them anything that they would not be receiving anyway. The only question was whether or not they would still take my class seriously; I was confident that they would.

I knew that I could not just walk into the room on the very first day of class and casually announce, "Hi, I'm your teacher! Everybody is going to get an *A!*" Instead, drawing upon an insight that I gained from observing Anna, I knew that I first needed to convey a sense that this was a serious course and that I was a serious teacher. I needed to lay the groundwork for my announcement. Therefore, I waited until the second class session to discuss my grading policy. I began by dividing my students into five groups and assigning each group a letter grade—*A*, *B*, *C*, *D*, and *F*. I told them their job was to brainstorm a list of words that they associated with their group's grade. For example, "What does an *A* mean to you? What does a *B* mean? and so on...." After the students had spent 10 or 15 minutes making their lists, I made five columns on the chalkboard—one for each grade—and asked a representative from each group to write their list of words in the appropriate column. We then studied the lists and looked for trends. For example, the *A* column contained words such as "excellent," "outstanding," and "brilliant," while the *F* column was filled with words ranging from "failure," to "stupid," to "no good." The other columns contained words whose connotations completed the continuum.

With these lists as our starting point, we then had a lengthy discussion about the role that letter grades had played in our own lives. The students spoke about instances in which they felt their grades had not reflected what they had truly accomplished in a course, and they told how grades had sometimes actually acted as an impediment to their learning. I, in turn, spoke of my own experiences as an elementary student and how my low grades had influenced my own self-concept. With this frank discussion laying the groundwork, I then explained that I *expected* to give everyone an *A* in the course, and I invited them to share their reactions. I asked them if they would work as hard without a letter grade to strive for. Would they spend less time on my course and devote more of their energy to other courses for which an *A* was not as certain? I made it clear that I was placing myself in a vulnerable situation, and that I was trusting them not to take advantage of me.[23]

Eliminating grades as an issue in this class proved to be a tremendously liberating experience—both for me and for the students. Throughout the semester, the students actually did more work, not less, and I developed a special bond with them that far surpassed any kind of relationship that I had ever managed to build with any of my classes in the past. They eagerly did their work because they felt a personal responsibility to me and to each other, not because they were working for a mere letter grade. At the end of the course, I gladly followed through on my promise and gave everyone an *A*, without the slightest feeling that anyone had not deserved it. Over the years, I have varied my grading policy from class to class—sometimes framing it as a *pass/fail* option in which students receive either an *A* or an *Incomplete*, while other times allowing the students themselves to decide how grading will be done. The important thing has been to challenge students' pre-conceived notions of assessment and to minimize the act of grading as much as possible within the institutional requirements established by my university.

My work with Anna has also influenced the kinds of assignments that we undertook in this class. Knowing Anna showed me that teaching is an autobiographical endeavor. It is autobiographical in the sense that the values and beliefs that guide teachers' actions are inevitably shaped by their personal histories. All of their past experiences—as children, as students, as preservice teachers, and as adults—play a significant role in determining the kinds of teachers that they become. Over time, I have come to realize that helping preservice and inservice teachers to discover the interplay between their personal histories and formal theories of teaching and learning is an important responsibility of teacher educators.

The way that I have tried to foster this connection between theory and personal histories in my own students is through autobiographical writing. One of my most effective assignments involves the writing of personal literacy autobiographies—that is, how we learned to read and write as children and the roles that reading and writing have played in our lives as we were growing up. I use the pronoun "we" because I participate too. Writing along with my students, I have produced a three-page autobiographical essay that I share with them (Muchmore, 2000/2001). Through this project, which ultimately results in the production of a class anthology, the class gains important insights into the literacy development of young children that we can draw upon in our later reading and discussion of more formal theories of literacy learning. In addition, because this activity involves writing multiple drafts, working in groups, and peer editing, I am implicitly modeling a way to teach writing. Thus, when we talk about writing instruction later in the course, we all share a common experience to which we can relate the theory.

In their papers, students have told stories about influential parents and teachers who helped them to become literate—as well as stories about hardships that they have to overcome. For example, one student told of growing up amidst the "unspoken family secret" that his father could not read or write, and how he had later helped his father to successfully complete a home course that was required for his job. He wrote,

> Why my father picked me to help him, whether or not I wanted to, out of five children, was not hard to figure out. I was the one who followed him to church when no one else was interested. I was also the one who admired his musical abilities so much that he taught me the basics of playing piano and guitar.

Speaking of the important role that music played in his relationship with his father, this student explained how he ultimately became an accomplished violinist, a minister of music in his church, and a middle school music teacher. For him, being literate involved an understanding of, and an appreciation for, music.

Another student, who was a foreign language major, wrote about the difficulty he had faced in learning Spanish. He explained:

> My experiences in Spanish were quite different from those that I had in English.... For the first time in my life I felt illiterate.... I wanted to be able to speak Spanish as well as I spoke English, but I couldn't. In fact, I probably never will.... Sure, I will one day be able to hold my own in conversations, or write an error-free letter, but I will never have the confidence that I have in English. I will never feel fully literate.

Still another student, in trying to explain her love for poetry and what it meant to her as a future teacher, wrote the following:

> Looking back, I realize how important language has been to me, to who I am. Reading and writing have, at times in my life, served as catalyst, treasure, escape, fortress, tool for con-

nection, and identity. I am my words, and that is ultimately empowering.... We are by nature language oriented beings—through language we communicate—not only with each other, but with ourselves. It is this importance which I hope to convey to my future students, in hopes that they my find a piece of the magic I've discovered....

When read as a whole, these class anthologies have served to illustrate the tremendous diversity of experiences within a class—and, by extension, have provided a vivid picture of the kind of diversity that preservice teachers might expect to encounter among their own students in the future. For example, in responding to the anthology created by her class, one student wrote:

> I have realized that each student will have a different background, different values and beliefs. As a teacher, I have to accept and try to understand where each of my students come from. I must figure out their background—what motivates each of them. It is hard to believe how closed my mind was only six short weeks ago. To think I have changed so much is wonderful. I have learned this through the anthology. Throughout my years of teaching, I hope I am able to expand my own students' minds so they can value and appreciate everyone in their own way too.

Another student explained:

> I feel that by reading the anthology and doing my own personal literacy history, I have a better understanding of what to expect as a teacher.... Even though all my students might be from the same area, society, etc., they will still be very different and unique.

Some students have stressed the cathartic value of reading the anthology, in helping them to deal with their personal fears and reservations about teaching. For example, one student wrote:

> The students I can definitely relate to are the foreign language students. They all expressed the fact that learning a foreign language is like learning to be literate all over again (except in a different culture)! One of my classmates ex-

pressed his frustration that he doesn't ever think he will be literate in Spanish.... Being a German minor, I feel that same way. I have an immense fear that I will never be a competent German teacher, because I do not feel that I am literate in German.

Another theme that has appeared in the students' written responses to their anthology involves insights about literacy. At the beginning of a semester, most students tend to define literacy solely in terms of one's technical competency in reading and writing—without appreciating the social, political, and personal consequences of these acts. In response to the anthology, however, a student expanded upon this initial conception as follows: "If I (now) had to define literacy, it would be... having the ability to successfully manipulate and comprehend the environment through the use of media skills such as reading, writing, speaking and listening." Another wrote:

> Reading through these entries it strikes me again and again; how many ways there are to learn, to think, and to define oneself. And, as we have discovered over and over again through the course of this class, how many ways there are to define literacy.

Still another explained:

> After reading the anthology, I have found that, as individuals, we all have (experienced) multiple influences shaping what we would consider to be our personal literacies. It seems that there is no one way to define what a personal literacy is, though all of our definitions seem to have roots in the principle that the way we learn is guided through these literacies. It is also common that literacy is defined as much more than the ability to read and write. In the anthology, I have found that some of us became literate through our environments, our hobbies, and values that our parents instilled in us. It goes without saying that our literacies define us. They tell us who we are, what we are, and why we do the things we do.

I always hope the assignment will foster this kind of reflection. However, it sometimes has another valuable consequence, which I value equally. Writing the personal literacy history papers and creating the anthology can transform a class—uniquely bonding the students and creating a tremendously positive classroom community. By sharing our personal stories, we have often come to know each other, and care about each other, in a way that transcends the kinds of superficial relationship that are typically formed in classroom settings. For example, a student once wrote:

> I was amazed how personal each story was and that we wanted to share with the class. Several people have commented on how we all feel like we have known each other most of our lives and it is true. We opened ourselves up through our writing.

Another commented, "It was a privilege to read these histories, and to hear those that were read in class. It was like a peek into our journeys, our pasts, and a tiny glimpse into our souls." One class even went so far as to plan and organize a group cookout and bonfire, entirely on their own.

Through this assignment, I consciously strive to create a sense of community among my students—a sense of shared responsibility for the class—which is in large measure a reflection of what I have learned from Anna.

Growing as a Researcher

I have learned a great deal through my work with Anna—both as a teacher educator and as a researcher. As a teacher educator, I have learned how to trust my students and support their learning in a way that is consistent with who I am as a person. As a researcher, I have learned that teachers' beliefs are complex and inter-related, and that we cannot fully understand these beliefs outside the context of the personal life histories in which they are imbedded. Surveys, such as the one I used in Kentucky, do not honor the complexity of teachers' beliefs or the contexts in which they are situated.

Ever since researchers in the field of reading first became interested in exploring the connection between teachers' beliefs and practices in the late 1970s and early 1980s (e.g., Barr & Duffy, 1978; Buike & Duffy, 1979; DeFord, 1985; Duffy, 1981; Hoffman & Kugle, 1982), survey-type instruments have been a common way to study teacher thinking. In fact, one of the more popular instruments, DeFord's (1985) "Theoretical Orientation to Reading Profile" (TORP), was still widely used by researchers wishing to characterize teachers' beliefs about reading in the mid to late 1990s (e.g., Evans, 1995; Ketner, Smith, & Parness, 1997; Morison et al., 1997; Sacks & Mergendoller, 1997). While I do not believe that there is anything inherently wrong with using surveys in general, I do believe that there are several significant shortcomings in using them to study teacher thinking.

First, survey instruments mute the voices of teachers by separating their beliefs from their lived experiences. Beliefs do not exist in a vacuum. They are formulated and are held by particular people in particular contexts—people who live and breathe, and have personal histories and future aspirations. All teachers possess life stories in which their thoughts and actions are situated. Yet, survey instruments such as DeFord's (1985) routinely filter out this rich and important contextual material, leaving only the disembodied responses to a series of propositional statements. Using surveys to study teacher thinking suggests a metaphor of beliefs as coins—coins that can easily be held and counted. After analyzing a collection of surveys, researchers confidently report that teachers believe "this, and this, and this," just as assuredly as they might announce that a person possesses three dimes, two nickels, and a penny. But beliefs cannot be held and counted like coins. Instead, they are more like the dancing shadows cast by the light of a fire. These shadows are in constant motion, continually blurring and melding to form an endless array of shapes and forms. Teachers' beliefs, like moving shadows, cannot be picked apart and studied in isolation without destroying the whole.

Second, there is a problem with validity. Survey instruments are far too rigid, forcing a person's thinking into pre-formed categories that do not necessarily represent what they actually believe. For example, my survey in Kentucky forced the teachers' thinking into a pre-existing conceptual scheme, which, although carefully conceived, probably did not fully represent their actual thinking. As I stated in Chapter 4, administering my survey was like pouring liquid plaster into a mold, allowing it to harden, removing the mold, and then announcing, "This is the shape of plaster." Like a mold, my survey had twisted and contorted the teachers' thinking into a series of ready-made categories. This simile was perhaps best illustrated through the remarks that some of the teachers wrote in the margins. Notations such as "Yes, but…" and "Sometimes" dotted the pages of their returned surveys, as they clearly struggled to make my pre-conceived categories fit their thinking. Other survey instruments—such as DeFord's (1985) "Theoretical Orientation to Reading Profile" and Duffy and Metheny's (1979) "Propositions About Reading Instruction Inventory"—also force teachers' beliefs into pre-existing conceptual frameworks. They parse teachers' beliefs, unnaturally separating them from the unique contexts in which they naturally reside.

Third, survey studies tend to encourage top-down models of change, offering well-intended policy prescriptions that unwittingly undermine teacher agency and erode their sense of professionalism. Because survey studies often deal with sizable populations and are more concerned with overarching trends than with individual cases, they are typically used to produce knowledge of a formally generalizable variety that is then forcefully applied to other teachers in similar situations. This authoritarian application of knowledge generally takes the form of top-down administrative mandates. For instance, when a researcher reports that a particular orientation to reading is associated with a particular way of teaching, there seems to be a natural tendency among policy makers to then attempt to effect wholesale change through mandates. I experienced this phenomenon in my Kentucky study when one of the reviewers of my study wrote, "The discussion should include mention of the need to provide district-sponsored and mandatory staff development." Although I successfully resisted this suggestion, I wondered how my study might ultimately have been interpreted by those who read it, and I held little confidence that my recommendations would not ultimately be translated into edicts anyway.

It is important to understand that I am not maintaining that all survey research is inappropriate and that it should never be used for any purpose. On the contrary, I believe that surveys can be very useful in certain instances, such as when researchers want to measure a simple construct and aggregate the data across a large population. Census taking is a good example of this kind of research. However, my study with Anna—combined with my experience in conducting a large-scale survey of Kentucky's Chapter 1 reading teachers—has convinced me that surveys are not well-suited for enhancing our deep understanding of how teachers think. Teachers' beliefs are far too fluid, interwoven, and complex to be measured through simple paper-and-pencil tasks.

Toward a Personal Theory of Teacher Thinking

My study with Anna represents an alternative approach to studying teacher thinking. Instead of relying upon surveys and questionnaires like DeFord (1985), Duffy and Metheny (1979), and others, my study relied upon a series of personal observations, one-on-one conversations, and other interactions with a single teacher conducted over an extended period of time. Characterized by an ethic of caring and sensitivity to the lives of teachers, my research is similar to the narrative work done by Clandinin and Connelly (1986, 1987, 1996, 2000), Connelly & Clandinin (1988, 1990), Elbaz (1983), Schubert and Ayers (1992b), and others.

However, it differs from their work in two important respects. First, it is more than just a narrative account of a teacher's life. It is a life history study, which means that the life has been situated within a specific context. This attention to context adds a depth and richness to the story, which enables a fuller understanding of the events and experiences that helped to shape it. Second, by situating Anna's story within my own autobiographical narrative, I have highlighted the transformative effect of doing this kind of research. Knowing Anna and studying her life has transformed the way I approach my work as a teacher, leading me to a personal theory of teacher thinking that has significantly influenced the way I approach my work with preservice teachers.

While my study with Anna is not appropriate for making statistical generalizations to larger groups of teachers, it *can* be used to build a theory of teacher thinking. Some researchers have a tendency to view teachers' beliefs as uni-dimensional and interchangeable entities that can be influenced through direct or indirect interventions (e.g., Bednar, 1993; Ginns & Watters, 1990; Laurenson, 1995; Lubinski, Otto, Rich, & Jaberg, 1995; Ojanen, 1993; Rueda & Garcia, 1994). The goal of such researchers, it seems, is to *change* the thinking of teachers in some way—a goal which they readily admit is extremely difficult to achieve. From my study with Anna, there emerges a theory that may explain this difficulty. I assert that beliefs are not uni-dimensional and interchangeable; instead, they appear on varying levels. For example, Anna's beliefs seemed to fall into two main categories—defined largely on the basis of their usefulness and longevity. On the one hand, there were transitory beliefs that arose primarily through her childhood experiences in school and her university experiences as a preservice teacher. These beliefs proved dysfunctional when she tried to put them into practice, and she therefore abandoned them. On the other hand, there were enduring beliefs that were, for the most part, deeply rooted in her personal life experiences that transcended school. These beliefs, which had withstood the test of time, were the very essence of who she was as a person, and they were virtually immutable to change. Over time, then, it was her teaching practices that gradually changed, as she made a concerted, career-long effort to develop a pedagogy that was consistent with her enduring beliefs.

The relative ineffectiveness of college experiences to influence the long-term thinking of preservice teachers has been well-documented. Zeichner and Tabachnick (1981) have observed that preservice teachers enter college with traditional notions about teaching and learning, temporarily become more progressive or liberal while in college, and then revert to their prior beliefs after they student-teach and enter full-time employment. Similarly, Holt-Reynolds (1992) has shown that preservice teachers often adopt the practices taught in their education methods courses without fully understanding or embracing the theories upon which they are based. They rely heavily upon their pre-existing belief systems, even though these systems may be diametrically opposed to the teaching practices which they are enthusiastically adopting. My personal theory of teacher thinking may help to explain this phenomenon.

If preservice teachers enter college with traditional attitudes toward teaching and learning, which gradually become more progressive while they are in college—but only temporarily—then perhaps it is because their teacher education experiences have not really challenged their existing thinking. My study with Anna suggests that authentic change occurs only when one's beliefs have been challenged in some way and found to be lacking. The responsibility of teacher educators, therefore, is to figure ways to highlight any acknowledged shortcomings and inconsistencies of preservice teachers' existing beliefs—not so that other beliefs can be mechanically inserted in their place, but rather as a form of self-discovery in which preservice teachers gain insights into their thinking and develop functional pedagogies that are both theoretically-sound and consistent with their innermost thoughts and feelings.

This theory of teacher thinking can also be used to explain my own development as a researcher. Through my work with Anna, in addition to other influences, I came to realize that when I shifted from survey methods to a life history approach, it was my practices that changed—not my underlying beliefs about research. Like Anna's beliefs about literacy, teaching, and students, my most basic beliefs about research have remained remarkably stable throughout my life. My current interest in life history research, for example, is deeply rooted in my early family experiences. When my sister and I used to sort through my grandmother's "trinket box," exploring the artifacts of our ancestors, we were actually doing research—although I did not consider it to be research at the time. Later, through my experiences as a student and a teacher, I developed a professional veneer of thinking that valued science over art and disregarded storytelling as a legitimate form of inquiry. Research was supposed to be cold, hard, impersonal, and objective—and researchers were supposed to approach their studies with intellectual engagement and emotional detachment. It took many years for me to gradually shed this professional veneer and move toward a research methodology that was consistent with my deeper and more personal understanding of research.

Conclusion

In the end, my study with Anna illustrates the tremendous complexity and contextualized nature of teacher thinking—a view which is seldom acknowledged through studies that rely exclusively upon survey instruments. In addition, this study reinforces the notion that being a teacher involves much more than simply mastering a set of skills. It also involves the development of an inner awareness—a sense of how one's life experiences have helped to shape the beliefs and underlying assumptions that ultimately guide one's practices. Most teachers seek a coherence between their personal theories of teaching and the practical demands of their jobs, but there is no single way to achieve this; there is no universal formula for success. Instead, I believe that teachers must ultimately develop their own personal pedagogies that are consistent with their inner selves. In this way, teaching is best viewed not as a science, but as an artistic form of self-expression.

APPENDIX

METHODS AND ETHICS
IN MY STUDY WITH ANNA

This appendix is divided into three sections. In the first section, I present a detailed inventory of all the information that I gathered in my study with Anna. In the second section, I describe the strategies that I employed in analyzing this information. In the third section, I discuss some of the ethical considerations that Anna and I encountered in our work together.

Sources of Information

The data for my study with Anna came from the following six sources: 1) fieldnotes; 2) interviews; 3) student writing; 4) Anna's papers; 5) archival information; and 6) personal experience. I describe each of these sources in greater detail below.

Fieldnotes

Following my 11 visits to Anna's classroom in 1992, I returned to her room 37 times during the 1993-1994 academic year—plus three times during the fall of 1994—for a combined total of 51 visits. The duration of my visits ranged from one class period to all day, and, with Anna's consent, I often came whenever my schedule permitted without always notifying her in advance. In my role as a researcher in her classroom, I typically jotted rough notes concerning my observations and impressions, which I then thickened afterwards. On days when I was heavily involved with individual students and did not have time to write fieldnotes on the spot, I sometimes used a small audiotape recorder to record portions of Anna's classes. Listening to these tapes afterwards was a useful way to reconstruct a days' events and produce detailed fieldnotes without having to rely solely upon my memory. I also used this tape recorder to preserve ideas or insights that I had when driving to and from Anna's school.

My presence in Anna's classroom seemed to cause little or no anxiety to Anna or her students. In other classrooms that I have visited over the years—both in Detroit and in other cities—I have often been greeted by an unspoken air of nervousness. "Who is this man and why is he here?" the students would silently wonder. Even after introducing myself and explaining the purpose of my visits, this tension would frequently remain. Anna's classroom, however, was different for several reasons. First, I was not the only regular visitor; other people from the University frequently came to her classroom too, which Anna welcomed. She viewed visitors as valuable resources for her students—people who could read her students' work, give them feedback, or otherwise contribute to the learning environment of the classroom—and, consequently, her students were quite accustomed to visitors. Second, Anna's students trusted her—both as a teacher and as a person—and because she presented me to them as her friend, they did not view me as a threatening person. Finally, because my visits were frequent, I got to know many of her students on an individual basis, so that their initial trust was strengthened by our subsequent interactions. The more they came to know me, the more they accepted me as a regular part of their classroom community and saw me as someone who could contribute to their learning.

Interviews

Much of the data that I collected was in the form of transcribed interviews. In addition to the two interviews that I conducted with Anna in 1992, I also formally interviewed her four times in 1993, once in 1994, and twice in 1995. The settings of these interviews varied. Four interviews took place in the English Department Office at Windrow High School; three took place in Anna's house; and two took place in my office at the University of Michigan. In addition, I had access to two transcribed interviews with Anna that were conducted by other researchers who were working with her on different projects. When combined into a single document, these 11 transcribed interviews spanned 299 pages, typed and single-spaced.

I also formally interviewed four people who had known Anna at various times throughout her career as a teacher—including a counselor, an assistant principal, a former professor whom I interviewed in 1992, and a former student of Anna, who was working as an English teacher at Windrow when I interviewed her in 1994. These interviewees were all suggested by Anna, who felt that they would know a great deal about her work as a teacher. In addition, in 1994, I had the opportunity to interview a former high-ranking official in the Detroit Public Schools, who provided me with historical information about the school and the neighborhood surrounding it. Like my interviews with Anna, each of these interviews was audiotaped and transcribed. Together, they filled 35 pages, typed and single-spaced.

Finally, during the spring of 1994, I interviewed 18 of Anna's current students, again audiotaping and transcribing each conversation. I selected these students largely on the basis of my pre-existing relationships with them, as well as their own recommendations. I initially approached students with whom I already had some kind of rapport and asked them if they would like to be interviewed for my study. I explained that I was interested in learning about their perspectives on Ms. Henson's teaching. Most of them said "yes" (only one student declined), and the interviews generally lasted 10 to 15 minutes. In order to expand my pool of interviewees beyond those whom I already knew, at the conclusion of each interview, I would ask the student to introduce me to someone else to interview next. This strategy proved useful, as I found it much less awkward to be introduced to a prospective interviewee by another student than to approach that person by myself. In addition to the 18 students whom I interviewed personally, I also gained access to three transcribed interviews with Anna's students that were conducted by another researcher who was working on his own project. Taken together, these 21 interviews spanned 86 pages, typed and singled-spaced.

In all of my interviews with Anna, her colleagues, and her students, I generally began with specific lists of questions that I wanted to ask—using these lists, however, more as personal memory aids than as rigid protocols for structuring the interviews. Most of the interviews—especially those with Anna—were more like informal conversations than formal question/answer sessions. They were characterized by a free flow of talk, with one topic leading to another, which led to another, and so on, until we might eventually find ourselves discussing ideas or topics that neither of us had anticipated. These kinds of spontaneous discussions often proved extremely enlightening.

Student Writing

In addition to the interviews, I obtained copies of reflective writing produced by all of Anna's students as part of their coursework. On the first day of school in 1993, Anna asked her students to introduce themselves to her in writing. She told them to be explicit about their concerns, their immediate goals for the class, and their future plans, and she invited them to ask any questions that they might have. After Anna responded to each student in writing—but before returning their papers—she and her students gave me permission to photocopy them. In addition, they permitted me to photocopy all of the completed mid-term and final examinations that were administered in January and May, 1994. Both of these examinations consisted of five essay questions requiring the students to reflect upon issues ranging from the quality of their work, to their growth as readers and writers, to their attitudes toward Anna's course, to their goals for the future. As a result, by June, 1994, I had accumulated 381 pieces of writing that were produced by 157 different students across all of Anna's classes. This writing, combined with the student interviews, helped to illuminate aspects of Anna's practices from her students' perspectives.

Anna's Papers

Another source of information was a collection of Anna's professional papers—including lesson plans, teaching documents, and academic papers that she had written throughout her career. Anna provided me with copies of all her lesson plans from the year in which I made most of my observations (1993-94), and she gave me one of her old lesson plan books from the late 1970s that she had found while going through some of her old work-related papers. Also among these papers, Anna found several past performance evaluations that were conducted by her immediate supervisors—both when she was a student-teacher at Windrow High School in the late 1960s, and when she was a beginning teacher at a Detroit junior high school in the early to mid-1970s. These evaluations included checklist ratings of her performance, as well as brief descriptions of the particular lessons that were observed. In addition, Anna shared many of her old teaching contracts and other professional papers that documented her career, including 19 academic papers which she had written for various graduate-level education courses during the 1970s and 1980s.

Archival Information

In order to understand the social, political, and historical contexts of Anna's career as a teacher in the Detroit Public Schools, I utilized archival information that I obtained from libraries and other sources. There have been many books written about Detroit, on topics ranging from the labor movement (e.g., Lichtenstein, 1995; Meier & Rudwick, 1979; Reuther, 1976), to the public schools (e.g., Irwin, 1973; Mirel, 1993; Rich, 1996), to youth gangs (e.g., Taylor, 1990, 1993), to race relations (e.g., Ezekiel, 1984; Katzman, 1973; Locke, 1969; Shogan & Craig, 1964; Widick, 1989), to the city in general (e.g., Chafets, 1990; Korab, 1992). Reading these kinds of texts helped me to understand some of the social and historical elements that led to the transformation of Detroit from a thriving manufacturing center in the 1940s and 1950s to one of most racially segregated and economically troubled cities in the United States in the 1990s. In addition, newspaper articles from the city's two major newspapers, *The Detroit News* and *The Detroit Free Press*, proved extremely valuable as a way to understand some of the local and national events that occurred between the 1960s and the 1990s which helped to shape the school contexts in which Anna's career was situated.

In order to learn about the history of Windrow High School, I relied upon a variety of sources, including past yearbooks dating from the 1950s to the 1990s. In addition, I located several important historical documents among the papers of the Detroit Urban League,[24] including an in-depth report on Windrow High School that was written in the late 1960s as part of a citywide study of all of Detroit's public high schools. This report—combined with the newspaper articles, the yearbooks, my interviews, and my personal observations—provided me with a rich understanding of the contexts in which Anna's teaching career unfolded.

Personal Experience

Finally, while working with Anna at Windrow High School, I also held a job with the Peace Corps Fellows Program at the University of Michigan, which provided me with much first-hand knowledge about life in the Detroit Public Schools beyond Windrow. Between 1993 and 1997, as a supervisor of beginning teachers, I made more than 200 visits to 26 different schools in Detroit—including seven high schools, five middle schools, and thirteen elementary schools. Drawing upon these experiences, in addition to my experiences as a participant-observer in Anna's classroom, I gained a keen understanding of the social, bureaucratic, and pedagogical challenges that Detroit teachers at all levels encountered in their work.

In fact, because of the wide range of schools that I visited, my perspective on the school district may have been more comprehensive than that of many people who actually worked there full-time. I make this claim because at the time of my visits the Detroit Public School District was divided into eight geographic Areas, each with its own superintendent and administrative structure. District personnel—including teachers, counselors, and school administrators—typically remained in the same Area throughout the duration of their employment. Rarely did they have the opportunity to work in or visit schools in other Areas. Even curriculum supervisors, who regularly traveled from school to school, seldom ventured outside the Area to which they were assigned. I, on the other hand, regularly visited schools at all grade levels across the entire District, thereby affording me a uniquely holistic perspective.

Analysis

Like many qualitative researchers, I was initially overwhelmed by the sheer volume of paper documents that my research generated. As the project progressed, my home became inundated by mounds and mounds of papers, some of which were eventually piled so high and balanced so precariously that the simple act of walking across the room would send them collapsing onto the floor. I needed a better system—one which would enable me to locate a particular document quickly without having to rummage through such huge piles of paper. To solve this problem, I divided my data into several broad classifications—such as fieldnotes, interviews with Anna, and student essays—and placed them into more than two-dozen three-ring binders, each with its own table of contents.

My next problem was how to quickly locate specific passages within the interview transcripts and other documents. Many times, while analyzing data, I could recall someone having said something in an interview but could not easily find it within a transcript. Sometimes, I spent several hours reading through all of my transcripts just to find a single relevant quotation. To solve this problem, I used my computer. Having already typed all of the interview transcripts on a word processing program and saved them as individual files, I found that by combining them into a single large file, I could use the "find" function to quickly scan the entire document for specific words. For example, if I could remember a quote, but could not recall who had said it or when it had been said, then instead of spending hours manually searching through volume after volume of printed transcripts, I could use my computer to instantaneously scan all of the transcripts for the key word or phrase. This way, I could usually find whatever I was looking for within a matter of seconds.

With the vast amount of data that I collected, there was also the problem of deciding what to include in my final report—and what to leave out. My initial impulse was to try to include everything. In the beginning, still heavily influenced by post-positivist notions about research that had been nurtured when I was in graduate school, I envisioned myself as a kind of container into which Anna was pouring out her story. I felt that it was my job to preserve and report everything exactly as I had received it. To leave something out, I felt, would be wrong. However, as my understanding of life history research grew, and my thinking became more consistent with what Denzin and Lincoln (2000) have called the "sixth moment of qualitative research," I realized that my container metaphor was highly inappropriate. Viewing myself as a mere receptacle for Anna's story implied a degree of precision and a degree of certainty in my work that simply did not exist. Anna's stories were much too fluid and changing for me to ever "capture" them in this way. No matter how hard I might try, they would always be incomplete; such is the nature of life history research (Cole & Knowles, 2001). Over time, I began to wonder whether it actually mattered if elements of Anna's story were left out inadvertently or deliberately? In both cases, something would still be missing—and I felt that it would be more honest for me to consciously edit Anna's story and reveal my criteria for doing so, than to naively present an inherently incomplete version of her life as if it were "the" definitive account.

Deciding what to include—and what to leave out

My criteria for deciding what to include in my account of Anna's story were based upon the following four questions that emerged throughout my work: 1) Is it relevant?, 2) Is it accurate?, 3) Is it necessary?, and 4) Is it ethical? Failing to find adequate guidance in the literature on life history research methods, I developed these criteria on my own as a pragmatic response to the massive collection of papers, fieldnotes, interview transcripts, and other documents that lay before me.

Is It Relevant?

In deciding what was relevant, I continually reminded myself of the purpose of the study, which was to understand Anna's beliefs and practices regarding literacy. Thus, I was able to eliminate much extraneous data, which, while interesting, were not directly relevant to the study. For example, I gathered a great deal of information about the history of Windrow High School and could easily have written dozens of pages about its evolution from a modern, orderly, state-of-the-art institution in the 1950s to an aging, underfunded, and sometimes chaotic building in the 1990s where the faculty regularly faced challenges that the school's early teachers could never have imagined. However, such detail would have been far beyond what was needed to establish the historical context of Anna's career.

Similarly, I could have explored issues relating to race and gender. For example, being a white researcher in a school where more than 99 percent of the students were African-American, I could have made race a primary focus of my paper. Or, being a male researcher working with a female teacher, I could have focused heavily upon issues of gender. I feel that both of these issues are very important and deserve to be studied.

However, because my work with Anna did not evolve from a point of view that was conspicuously rooted in either of these issues, I felt that it would be inappropriate for me to make them central to my research after the fact.

Is It Accurate?

In deciding what was accurate, I relied primarily upon my informed judgment, combined with input from Anna. One advantage of doing an in-depth interpretive study with one person which lasts for several years is that a researcher develops a heightened sense of what is true—an ability to see beyond initial impressions (Charmaz, 1995). By "truth," I am not referring to the correspondence of a set of facts to an objective reality that exists outside of human thought. Instead, I am referring to the correspondence of a set of facts to the subjective reality that was negotiated between Anna and me throughout our years of collaboration. And, beyond mere facts, I am referring to the internal coherence and consistency of her story and the extent to which it conveys some aspect of her persona. Does it sound like Anna? Does it accurately convey the mood of her classroom? Throughout our collaboration, these were questions that Anna herself helped me to answer.

Whenever I wrote something—whether it was fieldnotes, interview transcripts, or rough drafts of my paper—I always shared it with Anna and solicited her feedback. At the same time, however, I was mindful of her time constraints and the potential burdens posed by my requests. Thus, I generally left it up to Anna to decide how much she was willing and able to do, recognizing that there was a fine line between neglecting her input and demanding too much.

Is It Necessary?

In deciding what to include, I also continually asked myself whether or not particular pieces of information were necessary—both to the story that I was telling and to the overall quality of my writing. Because the effectiveness of interpretive research rests largely in the nature and quality of its presentation, I sometimes left out relevant and accurate information simply for the sake of rhetorical integrity. Paying careful attention to the craft of my writing, I tried to chose those stories or vignettes that best represented the developing themes that I had identified, and I attempted to weave them into what I hoped was rich and compelling prose. For instance, when I described Anna's life and career, I excluded a great deal of information that was redundant or might otherwise have detracted from the quality of my writing due to its sheer volume. With hundreds of pages of interview transcripts from which to draw, I had to be selective, choosing representative passages to exemplify particular themes rather than trying to include everything.

Occasionally, the information that I included was influenced by my own human limitations. On some days I simply had more time and energy to devote to my work, and the fieldnotes that I produced on these days tended to be more thorough and complete. Thus, while writing this book, I often included excerpts from these more polished fieldnotes, and excluded others, simply because the quality of my writing made it easier for me to incorporate them into my work. Nevertheless, I sometimes did go back and expand upon sets of under-developed fieldnotes—especially when they dealt with important themes that did not appear elsewhere in my fieldnotes in a more polished form.

Is It Ethical?

Finally, in deciding whether or not it was ethical to include something in my writing, I was guided by Kant (1785/1959), who maintains that we should always treat people as ends in themselves, never as merely the means to an end. Following this tenet, I tried to show the utmost respect for Anna, her students, and her colleagues. This means that I did not include personal information that might cause someone undue embarrassment, and I did not include personal information that Anna asked me to keep "off the record." I also excluded the gossip about teachers, students, and administrators that I overheard while visiting the school, even though much of it was quite interesting and was even relevant to my study. Throughout my work, I always placed ethical considerations above the criteria of necessity, relevance, or accuracy—reasoning that there were enough interesting, relevant, and accurate stories for me to tell without delving into issues that violated the mutual trust and respect that Anna and I had worked so hard to build and maintain.

However, such a stance raises an important issue. If I deferred to the participants in deciding what to include and what to leave out, then what prevents there from being a muted, distorted, and diluted version of events? What confidence do readers have that they are getting the "truth?" Ultimately, I decided that these kinds of concerns were unwarranted because they assume that there is only one way to tell a story. They assume a singular reality. I can tell a story that accurately conveys the tenor and ambiance of a situation without revealing *every* aspect of it with which I am familiar. As I learned throughout my work with Anna, it is impossible to record *everything*. Some things have to be left out, if for no other reason than there is not enough space to include them. Furthermore, I maintain that researchers' choices must be informed by considerations beyond mere editorial concerns. They must be informed by ethical considerations, as researchers meticulously weigh their obligations to the participants against those to prospective readers. In the remainder of this Appendix, I elaborate upon some of the ethical issues that are inherent in all life history and ethnographic studies and describe how Anna and I navigated them.

Walking an Ethical Tightrope

Unlike other forms of educational research, in which relationships between researchers and participants are characterized by business-like transactions that rarely extend into the realm of the personal, life history and ethnographic approaches can involve relationships that are both personal and complex. For example, what gave me the right to study Anna? Who was I to interpret her life as a teacher? What obligations did I have to Anna? ...to her students? ...to her colleagues? And what obligations did they have to me? These are some questions that I continually grappled with throughout the study.

There is no set of hard and fast rules for ensuring ethical behavior in life history and ethnographic research (see, e.g., Cassell, 1982; Cole & Knowles, 2001; Lincoln, 1990; Magolda & Robinson, 1993; Measor & Sikes, 1992; Punch, 1994). There are only guiding principles. Because ethical dilemmas are usually deeply embedded within the specific contexts of the situations in which they arise, what may be ethical behavior in one circumstance may not be ethical in another. For instance, it is not always ethical for a researcher to share with the participants everything that he or she had written, as I did with Anna. A colleague once told me of an ethnographic study that he conducted on the organizational management of a large company. He entered into this study with the promise that he would help the company by sharing whatever he learned. When it came time to disseminate his findings, however, he realized that some of the information he collected—while possessing a great deal of value to the existing research literature—had little or no potential value to the research participants. In fact, given the politics of the workplace, he felt that it might actually be harmful. It had the potential to cause ill-feelings among some of the company's employees and perhaps damage their working relationships. In the end, he decided to exclude this kind of information from the report that he shared with the company, while including it in an article that he later published in a scholarly journal. It was not an easy decision, he said. On the one hand, he felt ethically obliged to share "everything" with the research participants, while, on the other hand, he knew that such a stance was hopelessly naive. He chose a compromise—one which he hoped would preserve the work climate of the company while simultaneously serving his need to publish (in order to gain tenure and thus keep his own job).

The Value of Friendship

Anna and I began our collaboration as friends and colleagues and because our pre-existing friendship was based on ideals of honesty, parity, trust, and mutual respect, it was only natural that our research relationship continued with these same ideals. Anna was involved in every phase of the project, and we were fortunate to have never experienced any significant rifts in our friendship. Nevertheless, someone once asked me, "What if you had discovered during your research that you no longer liked Anna as a person? What if she had turned out to be completely different from the person you thought she was? What would you have done?" I responded,

> It definitely would have changed my research—and perhaps even ended it. I am certain that if Anna had suddenly made this same kind of realization about me, then she would definitely have ended it. Even if we had been able to work through such a problem, it certainly would

have changed the tenor of our relationship. It would
have been much more difficult for me to write about
Anna and share my work with her if I did not like her as
a person.

Lee (2001) describes this same dilemma in her ethnographic study
of an experienced elementary principal. While not basing her study on a
pre-existing friendship like I did with Anna, Lee did admire the principal
at the onset of her fieldwork, and tried to involve him as much as possible
in the research process. Over time, however, she was shocked to discover
that the principal was engaging in unethical and illegal behavior in his
job. She responded by adopting a critical stance in her study, which she
felt was within the bounds of the research relationship they had previously negotiated. The principal, however, felt threatened by these revela-
tions and began to avoid Lee. While not officially withdrawing from the
study, he did stop communicating with her—except to threaten a lawsuit
when she attempted to elicit his feedback on a preliminary draft. Lee
eventually completed the study, acknowledging that "both the researcher
and the researched had fallen short of (their) ethical ideals" (p. 71).

The Problem with Informed Consent

Recognizing the importance of maintaining an open and honest dialogue, Anna and I spent a great deal of time talking about the ethical
dimensions of my work. She once told me about a conversation that she
had with a mutual acquaintance whom we both knew professionally. Several months earlier, when my research was just beginning, I had told this
person about my work with Anna, and it had come up again in their conversation. Our friend was highly indignant about what I was doing. "How
dare he!" she had stated to Anna, wanting to know what gave me the right
to study Anna's life. Hearing about this incident forced me to stop and
think about a difficult question. What did give me the right to study Anna's
life? On one level, the answer rested with Anna herself. After all, it was
she who had given me the right to study her life. It was *she* who had
consented. But was her informed consent enough?

Under the guidelines of the National Research Act, a law first passed
by the United States Congress in 1970, researchers in the United States
are obliged to obtain the "informed consent" of those whom they study.

This means that researchers must tell their subjects, in advance, about the risks and benefits of their proposed participation and advise them that they are free to withdraw from the study at any time. To ensure compliance with this mandate, hospitals, universities, and other institutions require that all studies involving human subjects be submitted to specially-formed committees for approval. For me, this process involved the filling out of a rather lengthy form, which, unfortunately, was much more of a bureaucratic hurdle than a truly useful exercise.

The problem was that the process was based upon a model of research which did not honor the kind of relationship that undergirded my work with Anna. For instance, I was required to complete a questionnaire that asked, among other things, how I had recruited my subjects. "Be sure to specify the exact wording of requests, notices, or advertisements." Since I had neither "recruited" Anna in the sense that was implied by the question, nor did I regard her as my "subject" in a traditional researcher/ subject relationship, the question was inappropriate.

Another question asked me to indicate whether my study involved the use of deception, punishment, drugs, covert observation, physical harm, and so forth.... The list went on, dealing entirely with the most egregious kinds of unethical conduct imaginable—none of which were applicable to my situation. Far more relevant to my kind of study would have been questions such as the following: What information will you share with the research participants? What information will you withhold? Why? How will you resolve disputes if the participants disagree with your findings? Will you disseminate them above their objections?

Finally, the Committee wanted to see a copy of Anna's signed Informed-Consent Form—as if such a document was all that was needed for my study to be deemed "ethically correct." In research where direct human contact is usually minimal and there is a high degree of certainty about what will happen as the study unfolds, obtaining informed consent is relatively straightforward and unproblematic. Life history and ethnographic research, on the other hand, typically involve the establishment of deep and sometimes prolonged interpersonal relationships that continually change and evolve over time. In this kind of research, there is often a great deal of uncertainty about how a study will evolve and what kinds of risks the participants will ultimately face, and it is simply impossible to obtain informed consent through a single a priori encounter. Instead, as Cole and Knowles (2001) suggest, it must be continually nego-

tiated and re-negotiated in the context of a caring relationship between
the researcher and the participant throughout the entire duration of the
study.

Doing No Harm

In agreeing to collaborate with me in a study of her beliefs and practices, Anna made herself vulnerable to several levels of potential harm
against which I felt ethically obliged to protect her. It was conceivable,
for example, that my research could have undermined her relationship
with her students, created dissension among her colleagues, or even caused
her to lose her job. Throughout our work together, I attempted to minimize the potential for these kinds of harm. On the first day of school, I
introduced myself to each of her classes, telling them who I was and why
I was there. I also carefully explained my research to any of Anna's colleagues who inquired about my presence at Windrow High School. I
viewed myself as a guest at Windrow, and I made every effort to treat my
hosts—the students, the faculty, and the administration—with dignity and
respect.

However, as Cassell (1982) notes, harm in qualitative research is
most likely to occur not in the course of daily interactions between the
research participants, but in the course of writing and dissemination. When
I interpreted Anna's life, I may have done so with great respect and responsibility, but once my work has been disseminated, I have little control over how someone else might interpret or use it. People come to texts
with all kinds of prior conceptions and agendas, and they may inadvertently (or purposely) cause harm or discomfort to Anna. It is possible, for
instance, that she may be unfairly criticized—or she may be lauded as an
exemplary teacher, which is one outcome that she particularly wanted to
avoid. She made it clear that she did not want to be held up as an exemplar, and I tried not to present her in this way in my writing. However, my
good intentions will do little to prevent someone *else* from holding her up
as an exemplar, or criticizing her unfairly.

To mitigate these kinds of risk, Anna and I decided to use a pseudonym instead of her real name. Even though it may be a thin disguise for
her real identity, just by having a pseudonym, we felt that we would be
sending the implicit message to anyone who reads my work that Anna did
not seek attention—and we believed that readers would then have an ethical

responsibility to honor her desire to remain anonymous. While this stance may afford Anna some degree of protection from outsiders, we realized that the use of a pseudonym offers little protection to Anna, her students, or her colleagues from knowledgeable insiders. Colleagues, administrators, and other school personnel will ultimately know exactly who she is, no matter how well we try to protect her identity. Therefore, I depended greatly upon Anna herself to help minimize this risk. Because she knew the people and the politics of her work environment much better than I did, I relied upon her to critically read my work and tell me when she felt something might be problematic.

The Benefits of Anonymity

Anonymity has traditionally been viewed as a fundamental component of any research involving human subjects. Long perceived as a valuable instrument for protecting research participants against possible harm, it is typically offered almost as a "knee-jerk" action, with little or no thought given to the ultimate consequences. Recently, however, some researchers, such as Schulz (1997), have begun to question the practice of stripping research participants of their true identities and thus depriving them of any credit for their contributions. From this perspective, anonymity is seen as a pernicious tool for marginalizing research participants, and Shulz maintains that it is a "matter of ethics not to ensure anonymity, but rather to give full naming credit to the co-participants in a study" (p. 104).

Anna and I grappled with this dilemma again and again throughout our work together. The reason that we originally chose to use a pseudonym instead of her real name was to protect her, her students, her colleagues, and her school from potential harm. Initially, however, I was much more concerned about this than Anna. Not only was I concerned about the unknown risks that might emerge when my findings were disseminated, but I also felt that using a pseudonym was an important part of the research protocol—a well-established tradition that we ought not violate.

Over time, however, the issue became much more complex for us, and we vacillated. Did we really want use a pseudonym? Some of the early drafts of my work contained her real name, while others did not. Ultimately, we decided to stick with the pseudonym because we began to recognize that there were benefits to having anonymity beyond simply providing protection. For example, we recognized that using a pseudonym created a useful persona that enabled critique. Because of the fictive nature of life history research, lives are not simply recorded verbatim. Instead, they are created and interpreted for public critique. Through her pseudonym of "Anna," the real Anna became a fictive creation that could be interpreted and re-interpreted as a text. As "Anna," she is subject to any reader's interpretation and revision, and she is available for public critique. In contrast, the real Anna is not comfortable in this role, and she does not invite critique.

Anna once told me that she felt much more comfortable reading about "Anna" than reading about herself when I used her real name. She explained,

> You are creating the character that I play—the role that I have enacted as a teacher—but I am not limited by those descriptions. [Unlike "Anna"] I can continue to grow and change. My beliefs about literacy will continue to evolve [whereas Anna's will forever be frozen in the text].

In this sense, the use of a pseudonym empowered the real Anna to move beyond the "Anna" that I had created in the text. It enabled her to feel at ease in the way that I had characterized her in my writing. In addition, this distance between the fictive creation of "Anna" and the real Anna—and the comfort that it instilled in her—empowered me as a researcher. I felt like I could take more risks without thinking, "I don't want to show this to her. What if it hurts her feelings? What if she is upset by it? What if she is so offended that she quits the study?" Knowing that Anna felt removed from "Anna," enabled me to explore her life and career in ways that I would not have felt comfortable in attempting if we had been using her real name.

Conclusion

Unlike other forms of teacher research—which are based upon an objective, logical-deductive view of knowledge characterized by hypothesis testing and statistical analyses—life history and ethnographic approaches are consistent with the belief that teaching is a complex, personal endeavor shaped by influences beyond those which can be identi-fied through rating scales, surveys, and narrowly focused observations. Because life history studies typically involve the formation of human re-lationships that are far more complex than the limited, impersonal, busi-ness-like transactions that characterize traditional studies, their ethical dimensions cannot be effectively addressed through typical standardized procedures, such as simply using pseudonyms or obtaining the approval of an Institutional Review Board. Instead, ethical issues must be continu-ally dealt with at every phase of a life history research project, with the recognition that every study is unique and there are no universal prescrip-tions for ensuring ethical behavior.

ENDNOTES

1. A pseudonym. (p. viii)

2. Windrow (a pseudonym) is a comprehensive high school with an enrollment of approximately 2400 students, 99.5 percent of whom are African-American. (p. ix)

3. The term, "Chapter 1," refers to Chapter 1 of Title I of the Elementary and Secondary School Act of 1965, as amended by the Hawkins-Stafford Elementary and Secondary School Improvement Amendments of 1988. This legislation, which was originally part of President Lyndon Johnson's "War on Poverty," provided assistance to low-achieving students from low-income neighborhoods. In 1991, when I worked with Chapter 1, more than (US) $5-billion was provided to some 14,000 school districts to serve in excess of five million students (Fagan & Heid, 1991). This money was used for the design and implementation of supplementary programs in reading and math, the purchase of special instructional materials, and the hiring of additional teachers to meet the needs of "educationally deprived" children. Although the name of the law was changed from "Chapter 1" to "Title I" when it was amended by the United States Congress in 1995, I have chosen to use the old name here since it was in common usage at the time of my work in Kentucky. (p. ix)

4. William Tecumseh Sherman commanded the United States Army in the western theater of the Civil War. Famous for his phrase, "war is hell," Sherman captured and burned the city of Atlanta in 1864. Sherman's "march to the sea," which occurred shortly after the fall of Atlanta, involved a 300-mile campaign across Georgia that was designed to split the Confederate forces. Moving east from Atlanta to the coastal city of Savannah, Sherman's troops created a 50-mile wide swath of destruction, burning everything in their path. This tactic was considered extremely cruel and ruthless by many Southerners, and Sherman's name still evokes harsh feelings in the Old South. (p. 5)

5. NASA is an acronym for the National Aeronautic and Space Administration, which is an agency of the United States government. (p. 6)

6. There were 176 public school districts in the Commonwealth of Kentucky, two-thirds of which were county districts. The remaining one-third were called "independent" or city districts. Because the Independent districts encompassed relatively small geographical areas, usually cities within the counties, their enrollments tended to be limited. The county districts, on the other hand, typically drew many more students from much wider areas and consolidated them into larger, more comprehensive schools. (p. 14)

7. During the mid 1970s, Western Kentucky University was ranked as high as 8th in the nation in track and field, and 4th when the sports of track and cross country were combined (Nelson, 1976). (p. 16)

8. Peabody College for Teachers—previously known the Davidson Academy (1785-1806), Cumberland College (1806-1826), and the University of Nashville (1826-1875)—was a private school that merged with Vanderbilt University in 1979. Located immediately adjacent to the Vanderbilt campus since 1914, Peabody had enjoyed a close relationship with Vanderbilt prior to the merger. There had been joint academic programs and a joint library, and Peabody students had been allowed to participate on Vanderbilt's athletic teams. Nevertheless, there were also long-standing tensions between the students at the two institutions. As Conkin (1984) states in his comprehensive "biography" of Vanderbilt University, "Vanderbilt students had long taken a snobbish view of Peabody, sneer-

ing at its purportedly lower academic standing and at crip courses in education" (p. 714). Peabody students, in return, resented what they perceived to be the obnoxious arrogance of Vanderbilt students. According to Conkin, shortly after the 1979 merger, one Peabody graduate student bitterly expressed her attitude toward Vanderbilt by stating, "When I present my credentials a few years from now, I'd just as soon that no one know I technically graduated from the 'Harvard of the South'—where black students are mistaken for janitors, and frat boys who rate the bodies of passing women with large cardboard signs are considered cute and frisky rather than disturbed" (p. 714). This tension between Peabody and Vanderbilt students persisted after the merger and was still prevalent at the time of my visit in 1981. (p. 19)

9. I later learned that it was my mentor teacher who had urged the students to apologize. (p. 26)

10. This is the context in which my study with Anna originated. (p. 46)

11. See Note 3. (p. 59)

12. Closely related to this resurgence is the rise of narrative inquiry (see, e.g., Beattie, 1995, Casey, 1995, Connelly & Clandinin, 1990, 1991, Carter, 1993). Like life history research, narrative inquiry focuses on the stories that people tell in order to make sense of their lives. Narrative inquiry, however, focuses solely on stories without necessarily considering the social, historical, and political contexts in which they are embedded. Life history, on the other hand, refers to the in-depth study of a person's life story *and* the context in which in which it was experienced. (p. 64)

13. Recognizing the personal nature of Peter's work, I contacted him again via telephone on April 27, 1995, and received his permission to describe it here. (p. 72)

14. I draw this idea from the work of John Shelby Spong (1991), an Episcopalian Bishop who maintains that literal interpretations of the *Bible* trivialize the powerful experiences conveyed by those who wrote it. (p. 77)

15. It is important to note that I do not consider it to be ethical for a researcher to intentionally deceive readers by misrepresenting his or her work. Instead, my point is simply that the ultimate value of a story lies in the meaning that it has for individual readers, not in its literal correspondence to an objective truth. (p. 77)

16. In *Hooked on Books,* Fader, a professor at the University of Michigan, passionately outlined a comprehensive literacy program called "English in Every Classroom" through which he sought to instill in all children a love for reading and writing. (p. 88)

17. This assessment of Windrow was largely supported by other data, including school yearbooks, interviews with Anna, and informal conversations with other individuals who were familiar with the school during that time. (p. 89)

18. Early on the morning of July 23, 1967, the Detroit police raided an after-hours drinking establishment located in a low-income African-American neighborhood. A crowd gathered; insults were shouted; and a bottle was hurled through the window of a police cruiser. The situation soon escalated into a full-scale riot that lasted for six days. When it had ended, 43 people were dead, with more than 1000 injured and 7000 arrested. In addition, some 2,500 buildings were looted, burned, or destroyed, with property damage being estimated at $80-125 million (in 1967 US dollars). Altogether, it took more than 17,000 men to restore order to the city—including 4000 local and state police officers, 8500 Michigan National Guardsmen, and 4700 regular United States Army troops (Fine, 1989). (p. 92)

19. Vivian was another student seated at the table, who had read her own essay shortly before I entered the room. (p. 106)

20. I used a computer program called *FileMaker Pro* to assist in this analysis. My process was as follows: First, I created separate records for each piece of text that I had identified as containing one or more of Anna's beliefs. Next, I labeled each record with one or more themes that seemed to describe the belief or beliefs that they contained, and I sorted them electronically. To view all of the passages that related to a particular theme,

I used the "find" function to call them up as single document. This saved me the considerable burden of having to flip through hundreds of pages of text by hand, marking individual passages with colored pencils, cutting them with scissors, and manually sorting the clippings into piles. In addition, since I was able to include identifying information with each record, such as the date and page number of the full transcript from which a particular passage was taken, I was able to go back and forth between the specific excerpt and the full text whenever I had a question about the context from which the excerpt had been pulled. This enabled me to preserve the integrity of my data after it had been broken up and rearranged. (p. 119)

21. I do not mean to imply, in any way, that Anna discounted such theories. She had always been a serious reader and a scholar. Instead, I am merely asserting that her most basic beliefs about reading and writing were established primarily through her everyday experiences, rather than through her exposure to formal theories. (p. 119)

22. According to the principal, I was required to be in the room whenever students were present—and because there was at least one student assigned to my room at all times, this meant that I could never leave. (p. 136)

23. As a protective measure, I did maintain the right to give a student an "Incomplete" if he or she failed to come to class on a regular basis or did not do their best work. (p. 140)

24. These papers are located at the University of Michigan's Benton Memorial Library in Ann Arbor. (p. 154)

REFERENCES

Alcott, L. M. (1947). *Little women*. New York: Grosset & Dunlap. (Original work published 1869)

Anderson, R. (1977). The notion of schemata and the educational enterprise. In R. Anderson, J. Spiro, & W. E. Montague (Eds.), *Schooling and the acquisition of knowledge*. Hillsdale, NJ: Erlbaum.

Anne Frank in the World: 1929-1945 [touring exhibition]. (1987, January 19 through February 6). (Organized by the Anne Frank House, Amsterdam, and presented in Cincinnati, OH, by the Greater Cincinnati Interfaith Holocaust Foundation & the University of Cincinnati)

Asbjornsen, P. C., & Moe, J. E. (1957). *The three billy goats Gruff* (G. W. Dasent, Trans.). New York: Harcourt, Brace.

Ayers, W. (1992a). Teachers' stories: Autobiography and inquiry. In R. W. Wayne, J. W. Cornett & G. McCutcheon (Eds.), *Teacher personal theorizing* (pp. 35-49). Albany: State University of New York Press.

Ayers, W. (1992b). In the country of the blind: Telling our stories. In W. H. Schubert, & W. C. Ayers (Eds.), *Teacher lore: Learning from our own experience* (pp. 154-158). New York: Longman.

Ayers, W., & Schubert, W. H. (1994). Teacher lore: Learning about teaching from teachers. In T. Shanahan (Ed.), *Teachers thinking, teachers knowing: Reflections on literacy and language education* (pp. 105-121). Urbana, IL: National Council of Teachers of English.

Ball, S. J., & Goodson, I. F. (1985). *Teachers' lives and careers*. London, UK: The Falmer Press.

Barr, R., & Duffy, G. (1978, March). *Teacher conceptions of reading: The evolution of a research study*. Paper presented at the Annual Meeting of the American Educational Research Association, Toronto, Ontario, Canada.

174   *James A. Muchmore*

Beattie, M. (1995). New prospects for teacher education: Narrative ways of knowing teaching and teacher learning. *Educational Research, 37,* 53-70.

Becker, H. S. (1978). The relevance of life histories. In N. K. Denzin (Ed.), *Sociological methods: A sourcebook* (pp. 289-296). New York: Magraw-Hill.

Bednar, M. R. (1993, December). *Teachers' beliefs and practices: Dissonance or contextual reality?* Paper presented at the Annual Meeting of the National Reading Conference, Charleston, SC.

Bertaux, D. (Ed.) (1983). *Biography and society: The life history approach in the social sciences.* Beverly Hills, CA: Sage.

Bloome, D. (1985). Reading as a social process. *Language Arts, 62,* 134-142.

Bloome, D., & Green, J. (1984). Directions in the sociolinguistic study of reading. In P. D. Pearson (Ed.), *Handbook of reading research: Volume I* (pp. 391-421). White Plains, NY: Longman.

Blumer, H. (1969). *Symbolic interactionism: Perspective and method.* Englewood Cliffs, NJ: Prentice-Hall

Boon, J. A. (1986). Symbols, sylphs, and siwa: Allegorical machineries in the text of Balinese culture. In V. W. Turner & E. M. Bruner (Eds.), *The anthropology of experience* (pp. 239-260). Urbana: University of Illinois Press.

Bradley, L. (1981). A tactile approach to reading. *Special Education: Forward Trends, 8* (4), 32-36.

Brickhouse, N., & Bodner, G. M. (1992). The beginning science teacher: Classroom narratives of convictions and constraint. *Journal of Research in Science Teaching, 29,* 471-485

Bromme, R. (1982, March). *How to analyze routines in teachers' thinking processes during lesson planning.* Paper presented at the Annual Meeting of the American Educational Research Association, New York, NY.

Brown, R. H. (1987). *Society as text: Essays on rhetoric, reason, and reality.* Chicago: The University of Chicago Press.

Bruner, E. M. (1983). Experience and its expressions. In V. W. Turner & E. M. Bruner (Eds.), *The anthropology of experience* (pp. 3-30). Urbana, IL: University of Illinois Press.

Brunetti, G. J., & McCormick R. S. (2001). Guest editors' introduction: Lives of teachers. *Teacher Education Quarterly, 28* (3), 3-5.

Buike, S., & Duffy, G. G. (1979, April). *Do teacher conceptions of reading influence instructional practice?* Paper presented at the Annual Meeting of the American Education Research Association, San Francisco, CA.

Buswell, G. T. (1922). *Fundamental reading habits: A study of their development.* (Supplementary Educational Monographs, No. 21). Chicago: University of Chicago Press.

Campbell, D. T., & Stanley, J. C. (1966). *Experimental and quasi-experimental designs for research.* Chicago: Rand McNally.

Carter, K. (1993). The place of story in the study of teaching and teacher education. *Educational Researcher, 22* (1), 5-12, 18.

Casey, K. (1993). *I answer with my life: Life histories of women teachers working for social change.* New York: Routledge.

Casey, K. (1995). The new narrative research in education. *Review of Research in Education, 21,* 211-253

Cassell, J. (1980). Ethical principals for conducting field work. *American Anthropologist, 82* (1), 28-41.

Ceroni, K. M., Garman, N. B., Haggerson, N. L., McMahon, P. L., Piantanida, M., & Spore, M. B. (1996, April). *Disturbing our universe: The dissertation as personal narrative.* Symposium presented at the Annual Meeting of the American Educational Research Association, New York, NY.

Chafets, Z. (1990). *Devil's night: And other true tales of Detroit.* New York: Vintage Books.

Charmez, K. (1995). Between positivism and postmodernism: Implications for methods. *Symbolic Interaction, 17,* 43-72.

Clandinin, D. J. (1992). Narrative and story in teacher education. In T. Russell & H. Munby (Eds.), *Teachers and teaching: From classroom to reflection* (pp. 124-137). London, UK: Falmer.

Clandinin, D. J., & Connelly, F. M. (1986). Rhythms in teaching: The narrative study of teachers' personal practical knowledge of classrooms. *Teaching & Teacher Education, 2* (4), 377-387.

Clandinin, D. J., & Connelly, F. M. (1987). Teachers personal knowledge: What counts as 'personal' in studies of the personal. *Journal of Curriculum Studies, 19,* 487-500.

Clandinin, D. J., & Connelly, F. M. (1996). Teachers' professional knowledge landscapes: Teacher stories—stories of teachers—school stories—stories of schools. *Educational Researcher, 25* (3), 24-30.

Clandinin, D. J., & Connelly, F. M. (2000). *Narrative inquiry. Experience and story in qualitative research.* San Francisco: Jossey-Bass.

Clark, C. L. (1993). Teachers learning to teach: Stories teachers tell (Doctoral dissertation, University of Illinois, Urbana-Champaign, 1992). *Dissertation Abstracts International, 53,* 2332A.

Clark, C. M., & Peterson, P. L. (1986). Teachers' thought processes. In M. C. Wittrock (Ed.), *Handbook of research on teaching* (pp. 255-296). New York: Macmillan.

Cohen, R. M. (1991). *A lifetime of teaching: Portraits of five veteran high school teachers.* New York: Teachers College Press.

Cole, A. L. (1988, April). *Personal knowing in spontaneous teaching practice.* Paper presented at the Annual Meeting of the American Educational Research Association, New Orleans, LA.

Cole, A. L. (1989, April). *Making explicit implicit theories of teaching: Starting points in preservice programs.* Paper presented at the Annual Meeting of the American Educational Research Association, San Francisco, CA.

Cole, A. L. (1990a). Personal theories of teaching: Development in the formative years. *The Alberta Journal of Educational Research, 36,* 203-222.

Cole, A. L. (1990b, April). *Teachers' experienced knowledge: A continuing study.* Paper presented at the Annual Meeting of the American Educational Research Association, Boston, MA.

Cole, A. L. (1994, April). *Doing life history research—In theory and in practice.* Paper presented at the Annual Meeting of the American Educational Research Association, New Orleans, LA.

Cole, A. L., & Knowles, J. G. (1993). Teacher development partnership research: A focus on methods and issues. *American Educational Research Journal, 30,* 473-495.

Cole, A., & Knowles, J. G. (1995). A life history approach to self-study: Methods and issues. In F. Korthagen, & T. Russell (eds.), *Teachers who teach teachers: Reflections on teacher education* (pp. 130-151). London, UK: Falmer Press.

Cole, A., & Knowles, J. G., et al. (2000). *Researching teaching: Exploring teacher development through reflective inquiry.* Boston: Allyn & Bacon.

Cole, A. L., & Knowles, J. G. (2001). *Lives in context: The art of life history research.* Walnut Creek, CA: AltaMira.

Conkin, P. K. (1985). *Gone with the ivy: A biography of Vanderbilt University.* Knoxville, TN: The University of Tennessee Press.

Connelly, F. M., & Clandinin, D. J. (1984). Personal practical knowledge at Bay Street School: Ritual, personal philosphy and image. In R. Halkes & J. K. Olson (Eds.), *Teacher thinking: A new perspective on problems in education* (pp. 134-148). Lisse: Swets and Zietlinger.

Connelly, F. M., & Clandinin, D. J. (1988). *Teachers as curriculum planners: Narratives of experience.* New York: Teachers College Press.

Connelly, F. M., & Clandinin, D. J. (1990). Stories of experience and narrative inquiry. *Educational Researcher, 19,* 2-14.

Connelly, F. M., & Clandinin, D. J. (1991). Narrative inquiry: Storied experience. In E. C. Short (Ed.), *Forms of curriculum inquiry* (pp. 121-153). Albany: State University of New York Press.

Cook-Gumperz, J. (1986). Literacy and schooling: An unchanging equation? In J. Cook-Gumperz (Ed.), *The social construction of literacy* (pp. 16-44). Cambridge, UK: Cambridge University Press.

Cook. T. D., & Campbell, D. T. (1979). *Quasi-experimentation: Design and analysis issues for field settings.* Boston: Houghton Mifflin.

Craig, C. J. (1993). Coming to know in the professional knowledge context: Beginning teachers' experiences (Doctoral dissertation, University of Alberta, Edmonton, Canada, 1992). *Dissertation Abstracts International, 54,* 805A.

DeFord, D. (1985). Validating the construct of theoretical orientation in reading instruction. *Reading Research Quarterly, 20,* 351-367.

Denzin, N. K. (1989a). *Interpretive biography.* Sage University Paper Series on Qualitative Research Methods, Vol. 17. Beverly Hills, CA.

Denzin, N. K. (1989b). *Interpretive interactionism* (Sage University Paper Series on Applied Social Research Methods, Vol. 16). Newbury Park, CA: Sage.

Denzin, N. K., & Lincoln, Y. S. (2000). Introduction: The discipline and practice of qualitative research. In N. K. Denzin & Y. S. Lincoln, *Handbook of qualitative research, second edition* (pp. 1-28). Thousand Oaks, CA: Sage.

Diamond, C. T. P. (1991). *Teacher education as transformation: A psychological perspective.* Philadelphia: Open University Press.

Diamond, C. T. P. (1992). Accounting for our accounts: Autoethnographic approaches to teacher voice and vision. *Curriculum Inquiry, 22* (1), 67-81.

Diamond, C. T. P. (1993). Writing to reclaim self: The use of narrative in teacher education. *Teaching & Teacher Education, 9,* 511-517.

Dick, A. (1993). Ethnography of biography: Learning to live like a teacher. *Teacher Education, 5* (2), 11-21.

Dodge, R. (1907). An experimental study of visual fixation [monograph]. *Psychological Review, 8* (4, Whole No. 35).

Donmoyer, R. (1990). Generalizability and the single-case study. In E. Eisner & A. Peshkin (Eds.), *Qualitative inquiry in education: The continuing debate* (pp. 175-200). New York: Teachers College Press.

Duffy, G. (1977, December). *A study of teacher conceptions of reading.* Paper presented at the 27th Annual National Reading Conference, New Orleans.

Duffy, G. G. (1981, April). *Theory to practice: How does it work in real classrooms?* Paper presented at the Annual Meeting of the International Reading Association, New Orleans, LA.

Duffy, G. G., & Anderson, L. (1984). Teachers' theoretical orientations and the real classroom. *Reading Psychology, 5* (1-2), 97-104.

Duffy, G. G., & Metheny, W. (1979). *Measuring teachers' beliefs about reading* (Research Series No. 41). East Lansing: Institute for Research on Teaching, Michigan State University.

Duffy, G., & Metheny, W. (1978, November). *The development of an instrument to measure teacher beliefs about reading.* Paper presented at the Annual Meeting of the National Reading Conference, St. Petersburg Beach, FL.

Ebbs, C. A. (1996). Preservice teachers' literacy histories (Doctoral dissertation, University of Michigan, Ann Arbor, 1995). *Dissertation Abstracts International, 56,* 3085A.

Eisenhart, M. A., Shrum, J. L., Harding, J. R., & Cuthbert, A. M. (1988). Teacher beliefs: Definitions, findings, and directions. *Educational Policy, 2,* 29-50.

Eisner, E. W. (1991). *The enlightened eye: Qualitative inquiry and the enhancement of educational practice.* New York: Macmillan.

Elbaz, F. (1983). *Teacher thinking: A study of practical knowledge.* London, UK: Croom Helm.

Elbaz, F. (1991). Research on teacher's knowledge: The evolution of a discourse. *Journal of Curriculum Studies, 23,* 1-19.

Erickson, F. (1986). Qualitative methods in research on teaching. In F. Erickson (Ed.), *Handbook of research on teaching (3rd ed.).* New York: Macmillan Publishing Company.

Erickson, F. (1992). Why the clinical trial doesn't work as a metaphor for educational research: A response to Schrag. *Educational Researcher, 21* (5), 9-11.

Evans, A. D. (1995, February). *Bridging reading theory and practice: A study of lterns' beliefs.* Paper presented at the Annual Meeting of the National Association of Laboratory Schools, Washington, DC.

Everitt, B. S. (1977). *The analysis of contingency tables.* London, UK: Chapman and Hall.

Ezekiel, R. (1984). *Voices from the corner: Poverty and racism in the inner city.* Philadelphia: Temple University Press.

Fader, D. N. (1966). *Hooked on Books.* New York: Berkley.

Fagan, T. W., & Heid, C. A. (1991). Chapter 1 program improvements: Opportunity and practice. *Phi Delta Kappan, 72,* 582-585.

Faraday, A., & Plummer, K. (1979). Doing life histories. *Sociological Review, 27,* 773-798.

Fenstermacher, G. D. (1994). The knower and the known: The nature of knowledge in research on teaching. *Review of Research in Education, 20,* 3-56.

Filmore, C. (1947). *Christian healing: The science of being.* Kansas City, MO: Unity School of Christianity.

Filmore, C. (1953). *Keep a true Lent.* Lee's Summit, MO: Unity School of Christianity.

Filmore, C. (1960). *Mysteries of John.* Lee's Summit, MO: Unity School of Christianity.

Fine, S. (1989). *Violence in the model city: The Cavanaugh administration, race relations, and the Detroit riot of 1967.* Ann Arbor: The University of Michigan Press.

Firestone, W. A. (1993). Alternative arguments for generalizing from data as applied to qualitative research. *Educational Researcher, 22* (4), 16-23.

Fischer, L. R. (1983). Sociology and life history: Methodological incongruence? *International Journal of Oral History, 4,* 29-40.

Fish, S. (1980). *Is there a text in this class? The authority of interpretive communities.* Cambridge, MA: Harvard University Press.

Fishman, A. R. (1987). Literacy and cultural context: A lesson from the Amish. *Language Arts, 64,* 842-854.

Fishman, A. R. (1988). *Amish literacy: What and how it means.* Portsmouth, NH: Heinemann.

Fiske, E. B. (1988). *The Fiske guide to colleges.* New York: Times Books.

Frank, A. (1983). *Anne Frank's tales from the secret annex* (R. Manheim, & M. Mok, Trans.). New York: Washington Square Press.

Freire, P. & Macedo, D. (1987). *Literacy: Reading the world and the word.* South Hadley, MA: Bergin & Garvey.

Friedenberg, E. Z. (1964). *The vanishing adolescent.* Boston: Beacon Press.

Geertz, C. (1973). *The interpretation of cultures: Selected essays.* New York: Basic Books.

Geertz, C. (1983). *Local knowledge: Further essays in interpretive anthropology.* New York: Basic Books.

Gies, M., with Gold, A. L. (1987). *Anne Frank remembered: The story of the woman who helped to hide the Frank Family.* New York: Simon and Schuster.

Gilmore, J. V., & Gilmore, E. C. (1968). *Gilmore oral reading test.* New York: Harcourt Brace Javonovich.

Ginns, I. S., & Watters, J. J. (1990). *A longitudinal study of preservice elementary teachers' personal and science teaching efficacy* (Technical Report). (ERIC Document Reproduction Service No. ED 404 127)

Giroux, H. A. (1988). Literacy and the pedagogy of voice and political empowerment. *Educational Theory, 38,* 61-75.

Goethe, J. W. (1941). *Faust.* New York: Knopf. (Original work published 1808-1832)

Goodman, K. S. (1969). Analysis of oral reading miscues: Applied psycholinguistics. *Reading Research Quarterly, 5,* 9-30.

Goodman, K. S. (1976). Behind the eye: What happens in reading. In H. Singer & R. B. Ruddell (Eds.), *Theoretical models and processes of reading* (pp. 509-535). Newark, DE: International Reading Association.

Goodman, P. (1964). *Compulsory mis-education.* New York: Horizon Press.

Goodrich, F., & Hackett, A. (1956). *The diary of Ann Frank.* New York: Random House.

Goodson, I. (Ed.) (1992). *Studying teachers' lives.* New York: Teachers College Press.

Goodson, I., & Cole, A. (1993). Exploring the teacher's professional knowledge. In D. McLaughlin, & W. G. Tierney (Eds.), *Naming si-*

lenced lives: Personal narratives and processes of educational change (pp. 71-94). New York: Routledge.

Gough, P. C. (1976). One second of reading. In J. F. Kavanagh & I. G. Mattingly (Eds.), *Language by ear and eye* (pp. 331-358). Cambridge, MA: MIT Press.

Gove, M. K. (1983). Clarifying teachers' beliefs about reading. *The Reading Teacher, 37*(3), 261-268.

Greene, M. (1982). Literacy for what? *Visible language, 26,* 77-86.

Greene, M. (1990, January 16). *Tensions and openings: Landscapes for the future.* Address delivered at Eastern Michigan University, Ypsilanti, MI.

Griffin, P. (1977). How and when does reading occur in the classroom? *Theory into practice, 16,* 376-382.

Grossman, P. L. (1990). *The making of a teacher: Teacher knowledge and teacher education.* New York: Teachers College Press.

Grossman, P. L. (1991). The selection and organization of content for secondary English: Sources for teachers' knowledge. *English Education, 23* (1), 39-53.

Grumatky, H. (1967). *Little Toot.* New York: Putnam.

Guba, E. G., & Lincoln, Y. S. (1989). *Personal communication.* Beverly Hills, CA: Sage.

Gudmundsdottir, S. (1987a). Ways of seeing are ways of knowing: The knowledge of an expert English teacher. *Journal of Curriculum Studies, 23* (5), 409-421.

Gudmundsdottir, S. (1987b, April). *Learning to teach social studies: Case studies of Chris and Cathy.* Paper presented at the Annual Meeting of the American Educational Research Association, Washington, DC.

Gudmundsdottir, S. (1987c, April). *Pedagogical content knowledge: Teachers' ways of knowing.* Paper presented at the Annual Meeting of the American Educational Research Association, Washington, DC.

Gudmundsdottir, S. (1989). Knowledge use among experienced teachers: Four case studies of high school teaching. (Doctoral dissertation, Stanford University, San Francisco, CA, 1988). *Dissertation Abstracts International, 49,* 3688A.

Gudmundsdottir, S. (1990). Values in pedagogical content knowledge. *Journal of Teacher Education, 41* (3), 44-52.

Gudmundsdottir, S. (1992, April). *The interview as a joint construction of reality.* Paper presented at the Annual Meeting of the American Educational Research Association, San Francisco, CA.

Gustafson, G. L. (1995). Teachers' assumptions, beliefs and values about teaching spelling: A study of teacher development (Master thesis, Simon Fraser University, British Columbia, Canada, 1993). *Masters abstracts international, 33,* 314.

Hall, M. (1981). *Teaching reading as a language experience.* Columbus, OH: Charles E. Merrill Co.

Hall, S., & Grant, G. E. (1991). On what is known and seen: A conversation with a research participant. *Journal of Curriculum Studies, 23,* 423-428.

Harste, J. C., & Burke, C. L. (1977). A new hypothesis for reading teacher research: Both *teaching* and *learning* of reading are theoretically based. In P. D. Pearson (Ed.), *Reading theory research and practice,* Twenty-sixth Yearbook of the National Reading Conference (pp. 32-40). Clemsen, SC: National Reading Conference.

Harste, J. C., Woodward, V. A., & Burke, C. L. (1984). Examining our assumptions: A transactional view of literacy and learning. *Research in the Teaching of English, 18,* 84-108.

Heath, S. B. (1983). *Ways with words: Language, life and work in communities and classrooms.* Cambridge, UK: Cambridge University Press.

Heath, S. B. (1991). The sense of being literate: Historical and cross-cultural features. In R. Barr, M. L. Kamil, P. B. Mosenthal, & P. D. Pearson (Eds.), *Handbook of reading research: Volume II* (pp. 3-25). New York: Longman.

High School Study Commission (1967). *Report of findings and recommendations.* Detroit, MI: author. (located in Detroit Urban League Papers, Bentley Historical Library, University of Michigan, Ann Arbor)

Hoffman, J. V., & Kugle, C. L. (1982). A study of theoretical orientation to reading and its relationship to teacher verbal feedback during reading instruction. *Journal of Classroom Interaction, 18,* 2-7.

Holland, N. N. (1980). Unity identity text self. In J. P. Tompkins (Ed.), *Reader-response criticism: From formalism to post-structuralism* (pp. 118-133). Baltimore: The Johns Hopkins University Press.

Holmes, J. A. (1953). *The substrata-factor theory of reading.* Berkely, CA: Berkeley Book Company.

Holt, J. C. (1964). *How children fail.* New York: Pitman.

Holt, J. C. (1967). *How children learn.* New York: Pitman.

Holt, J. C. (1981). *Teach your own: A hopeful path for education.* New York: Delacorte Press.

Holt-Reynolds, D. (1992). Personal history based beliefs as relevant prior knowledge in course work. *American Educational Research Journal, 29,* 325-349.

Holt-Reynolds, D. (1994). When agreeing with the professor is bad news for preservice teacher educators: Jeanneane, her personal history, and coursework. *Teacher Education Quarterly, 21,* 13-35.

Illich, I. (1971). *Deschooling society.* New York: Harper & Row.

Illich, I. (1973). *After deschooling, what?* New York: Harper & Row.

Irwin, J. R. (1973). *A ghetto principal speaks out: A decade of crisis in urban public schools.* Detroit, MI: Wayne Sate University Press.

Iser, W. (1978). *The act of reading: A theory of aesthetic response.* Baltimore: The Johns Hopkins University Press.

Janesick, V. (1978). *An ethnographic study of a teacher's classroom perspective: Implications for curriculum.* East Lansing, MI: Institute for Research on Teaching.

Javel, E. (1879). Essai sur la physiologie de la lecture. *Annales d'oculistique, 82,* 242-253.

Johnson, J. (1988). The relationship between preservice reading teachers' instruction of reading their emerging conceptions of reading. In J. E. Readence, R. S. Baldwin, J. P. Konopak, & P. R. O'Keefe (Eds.), *Dialogues in literacy research,* thirty-seventh yearbook of the National Reading Conference (pp. 355-361). Chicago: The National Reading Conference.

Johnson, K. E. (1992). The relationship between teachers' beliefs and practices during literacy instruction for non-native speakers of English. *Journal of Reading Behavior, 24,* 83-108.

Jung, C. G. (1939). *Modern man in search of a soul* (W. S. Dell & C. F. Baynes, Trans.). New York: Harcourt, Brace.

Jung, C. G. (1957). *The undiscovered self* (R. F. C. Hull, Trans.). New York: Little, Brown.

Jung, C. G. (1958). *Psyche and symbol* (V. S. de Laszlo, Ed.). Garden City, NY: Doubleday.

Kagan, D. M. (1992). Implications of research on teacher belief. *Educational Psychologist, 27,* 65-90.

Kagan, D. M., & Tippins, D. J. (1991). How teachers' classroom cases express their pedagogical beliefs. *Journal of Teacher Education, 42,* 281-291.

Kamil, M. L., & Pearson, D. (1979). Theory and practice in teaching reading. *New York University Education Quarterly, 10* (2), 10-16.

Kant, I. (1959). *Foundations of the metaphysics of morals* (L. W. Beck, Trans.). Indianapolis, IN: Bobbs-Merrill. (Original work published in 1785)

Katzman (1973). *Before the Ghetto: Black Detroit in the nineteenth century.* Urbana, IL: University of Illinois Press.

Ketner, C. S., Smith, K. E., & Parness, M. K. (1997). Relationship between teacher theoretical orientation to reading and endorsement of developmentally appropriate practice. *Journal of Educational Research, 90* (4), 212-220.

Kinzer, C. K., & Carrick, D. A. (1986). Teacher beliefs as instructional influences. In J. A. Niles & R. V. Lalik (Eds.), *Solving problems in literacy: Learners, teachers and researchers,* Thirty-fifth Yearbook of the National Reading Conference (pp. 127-134). Rochester, NY: The National Reading Conference.

Kirk, J., & Miller, M. L. (1986). *Reliability and validity in qualitative research* (Sage University Paper Series on Qualitative Research Methods, Vol. 1). Beverly Hills, CA: Sage.

Knowles, J. G. (1993). Life-history accounts as mirrors: A practical avenue for the conceptualization of reflection in teacher education. In J. Calderhead & P. Gates (Eds.), *Conceptualizing reflection in teacher development* (pp. 70-98). London, UK: Falmer Press.

Knowles, J. G., & Muchmore, J. A. (1995). Yep! We're grown up home schooled kids—and we're doing just fine, thank you. *Journal of Research on Christian Education, 4* (1), 35-56.

Knowles, J. G., Marlow, S., & Muchmore, J. (1992). From Pedagogy to ideology: Origins and phases of the home education movement in the United States, 1970-1990. *American Journal of Education, 100* (2), 195-235.

Koivu-Rybicki, V. T. (1996). Examining a teaching life: Stories of experience as epiphanies. (Doctoral dissertation, University of Michigan, Ann Arbor, 1995). *Dissertation Abstracts International, 57,* 4653A.

Korab, B. (1992). *Detroit: The Renaisance city.* Columbiaville, MI: Spradlin.

Kvale, S. (1989). To validate is to question. In S. Kvale (Ed.), *Issues of validity in qualitative research* (pp. 73-92). Lund, Sweden: Studentlitteratur.

Lakoff, G., Johnson, M. (1980). *Metaphors we live by*. Chicago: University of Chicago Press.

Laurenson, D. J. (1995). Mathematics and the drift toward constructivism: Are teacher beliefs and teaching practice following the beat of the same drummer? *NCSSSMST Journal, 1* (2), 3-7.

Lee, D. J. (Ed.) (1994). *Life and story: Autobiographies for a narrative psychology*. Wesport, CT: Praeger.

Lee, S. S. (2001). "A root out of a dry ground": Resolving the researcher/ researched dilemma. In J. Zeni (Ed.), *Ethical issues in practitioner research* (pp. 61-71). New York: Teachers College Press.

Lenzo, P. (1992, April 4). Master of Fine Arts Exhibit, Wayne State University, Detroit, MI.

Li, X. (2002). *The tao of life stories: Chinese language, poetry, and culture in education*. New York: Peter Lang.

Lichtenstein, N. (1995). *The most dangerous man in Detroit: Walter Reuther and the fate of American labor*. New York: Basic Books.

Lincoln, Y. S. (1990). Toward a categorical imperative for qualitative research. In E. W. Eisner, & A. Peshkin (Eds.), *Qualitative inquiry in education: The continuing debate* (pp. 277-295). New York: Teachers College Press.

Locke, H. G. (1969). *The Detroit riot of 1967*. Detroit, MI: Wayne State University Press.

Loughran, J., & Russell, T. (1997). *Teaching about teaching: Purpose, passion and pedagogy in teacher education*. London, UK: Falmer.

Lubinski, C. A., Otto, A., Rich, B. S., & Jaberg, P. A. (1995, October). *Content knowledge, beliefs, and Practices: A comparison among six preservice teachers*. Paper presented at the Annual Meeting of the North American Chapter of the International Group for the Psychology of Mathematics Education, Columbus, OH.

Mackey, R. (1966, April 8). 2,300 picket at Northern; Brownell grants demands. *Detroit Free Press*, pp. 1A, 4A.

Magolda, P. M., & Robinson, B. M. (1993, April). *Doing harm: Unintended consequences of fieldwork*. Paper presented at the Annual Meeting of the American Educational Research Association, Atlanta, GA.

Mahabir, H. (1993). Autobiography as a way of knowing. In D. J. Clandinin, A. Davies, P. Hogan, & B. Kennard (Eds.), *Learning to teach, teaching to learn: Stories of collaboration in teacher education* (pp. 19-27). New York: Teachers College Press.

Marland, P. (1977). *A study of teachers' interactive thoughts.* Unpublished doctoral dissertation, University of Alberta, Edmonton, Canada.

McCallister, C. (1998). *Reconceptualizing literacy methods instruction: To build a house that remebers its forest.* New York: Peter Lang.

McNinch, G. A. (1981). A method for teaching sight words to disabled readers. *The Reading Teacher, 35* (3), 269-272.

Measor, L., & Sikes, P. (1992). Visiting lives: Ethics and methodology in life history. In I. F. Goodson (Ed.), *Studying teachers' lives* (pp. 209-233). London, UK: Routledge.

Medway, F. J. (1979). Causal attributes for school-related problems: Teacher perceptions and teacher feedback. *Journal of Educational Psychology, 71,* 809-818.

Meier, A., & Rudwick, E. (1979). *Black Detroit and the rise of the UAW.* New York: Oxford University Press.

Melnick, C. R. (1992). The out-of-school curriculum: An invitation, not an inventory. In W. H. Schubert, & W. C. Ayers (Eds.), *Teacher lore: Learning from our own experience* (pp. 81-106). New York: Longman.

Merton, T. (1948). *The seven story mountain.* New York: Harcourt, Brace.

Merton, T. (1949). *Seeds of contemplation.* Norfolk, CT: New Directions Books.

Miller, J. L. (1992). Teachers' spaces: A personal evolution of teacher lore. In W. H. Schubert, & W. C. Ayers (Eds.), *Teacher lore: Learning from our own experience* (pp. 11-24). New York: Longman.

Millies, P. S. G. (1992). The relationship between a teacher's life and teaching. In W. H. Schubert, & W. C. Ayers (Eds.), *Teacher lore: Learning from our own experience* (pp. 25-43). New York: Longman.

Mirel, J. (1993). *The rise and fall of an urban school system: Detroit, 1907-81.* Ann Arbor, MI: The University of Michigan Press.

Mishler, E. (1990). Validation in inquiry-guided research: The role of exemplars in narrative studies. *Harvard Educational Review, 60,* 415-442.

Moilanen, M. B. (1990). Identifying teachers' concepts of art history in secondary school art programs (Doctoral dissertation, The University of Wisconsin, Madison, 1989). *Dissertation Abstracts International, 50,* 3453-A.

Morison, T. G., Wilcox, B., Madrigral, J. L., & McEwan, B. (1997). Development of teachers' theoretical orientations toward reading and pupil control ideology. *Reading Research and Instruction, 36* (2), 141-156.

Muchmore, J. A. (1994). A Statewide survey of the beliefs and practices of Chapter 1 reading teachers. *Remedial and Special Education, 15* (4), 252-259.

Muchmore, J. A., & Knowles, J. G. (1993, April). *Initiating change through a professional Development school: Three teachers' experiences.* Paper presented at the Annual Meeting of the American Educational Research Association, Atlanta, GA.

Muchmore, J. A. (2000/2001). Reflections on literacy and teaching: A personal story. *Journal of Adolescent and Adult Literacy , 44* (4), 332-334.

Munby, H. (1982). The place of teachers' beliefs in research on teacher thinking and decision making, and an alternative methodology. *Instructional Science, 11,* 201-225.

Munby, H. (1985, April). *Teachers' professional knowledge: A study of metaphor.* Paper presented at the Annual Meeting of the American Educational Research Association, Chicago, IL.

Munby, H. (1986). Metaphor in the thinking of teachers: An exploratory study. *Journal of Curriculum Studies, 18,* 197-209.

Munby, H. (1987a). Metaphor and teachers' knowledge. *Research in the Teaching of English, 21* (4), 377-397.

Munby, H. (1987b, April). *Metaphorical expressions of teachers' practical curriculum knowledge.* Paper presented at the Annual Meeting of the American Educational Research Association, Washington, DC.

Munby, H. (1987c, April). *Metaphors, puzzles, and teachers' professional knowledge.* Paper presented at the Annual Meeting of the American Educational Research Association, Washington, DC.

Munby, H. (1990). Metaphorical expressions of teachers' practical curriculum knowledge. *Journal of Curriculum and Supervision, 6* (1), 18-30.

Munby, H., & Russell, T. (1989, April). *Metaphor in the study of teachers' professional knowledge.* Paper presented at the Annual Meeting of the American Educational Research Association, San Francisco, CA.

Neill, A. S. (1960). *Summerhill: A radical approach to child rearing.* New York: Hart.

Neilsen, L. (1989). *Literacy and living: The literate lives of three adults.* Portsmouth, NH: Heinemann.

Neilsen, L. (1998). *Knowing her place: Research literacies and feminist occasions.* Great Tancook Island, Nova Scotia, Canada: Backalong Books. San Francisco, CA: Caddo Gap Press. (co-publishers)

Nelson, B. (1976, February). Of people & things. *Track & Field News, 29,* 53.

Nespor, J. & Barylske, J. (1991). Narrative discourse and teacher knowledge. *American Educational Research Journal, 28,* 805-823.

Ojanen, S. (1993, June). *A process in which personal pedagogical knowledge is created through the teacher education experience.* Paper presented at the International Conference in Teacher Education, Tel-Aviv, Israel.

Olson, M. R. (1995). Narrative authority in (teacher) education (Doctoral dissertation, University of Alberta, Edmonton, Canada, 1993). *Dissertation Abstracts International, 55,* 1918A.

One protest by students which deserves applause [editorial] (1966, April 9). *Detroit Free Press,* p. 6A.

Oppenheimer, J., Carroll, B., & Pugh, M. (1952). Job Switching (W. Asher, Director). In J. Oppenheimer (Producer), *I Love Lucy.* New York: Columbia Broadcasting System.

Pearson, P. D. (1974). The effects of grammatical complexity on children's comprehension, recall and conception of certain semantic relations. *Reading Research Quarterly, 10,* 155-192.

Peshkin, A. (1986). *God's choice: The total world of a fundamentalist Christian school.* Chicago: University of Chicago Press.

Philion, T. (1998). Three codifications of critical literacy. In C. Fleischer & D. Schaafsma (Eds.), *Literacy and democracy: Teacher research and composition studies in pursuit of habitable spaces* (pp. 53-81). Urban, IL: National Council of Teachers of English.

Piper, W. (1961). *The little engine that could.* New York: Platt & Munk. (Original work published 1930)

Plofchan, F. (Photographer) (1966, April 8). Northern High School students walked out in protest. *Detroit Free Press,* p. 1A.

Polkinghorne, D. E. (1988). *Narrative knowing and the human sciences.* Albany, NY: State University of New York Press.

Ponticell, J. A. (1993, April). *Research into the nature of teachers' beliefs about teaching: A study of exemplary and marginal teachers.* Paper presented at the Annual Meeting of the American Educational Research Association, Atlanta, GA.

Punch, M. (1994). Politics and ethics in qualitative research. In N. K. Denzin, & Y. S. Lincoln (Eds.), *Handbook of qualitative research* (pp. 83-97). Thousand Oaks, CA: Sage.

Randall, W. L. (1995). *The stories we are: An essay in self-creation.* Toronto, Canada: University of Toronto Press.

Resnais, A. (Director). (1955). *Night and fog* [film]. (Released in the U. S. by Contemporary Films/McGraw-Hill)

Reuther, V. G. (1976). *The brothers Ruether and the story of the UAW.* Boston: Houghlin Mifflin.

Rich, W. C. (1996). *Black mayors and school politics: The failure of reform in Detroit, Gary, and Newark.* New York: Garland.

Richardson, V., Anders, P., Tidwell, D., & Lloyd, C. (1991). The relationship between teachers' beliefs and practices in reading comprehension instruction. *American Educational Research Journal, 28,* 559-586.

Roberts, P. (1968). *The Robert's English series: A linguistic program.* New York: Harcourt, Brace, & World.

Rogers, C. R. (1969). *Freedom to learn: A view of what education might become.* Columbus, OH: Merrill.

Rosoff, B. L., Woolfolk, A. E., & Hoy, W. K. (1991, April). *Teachers' beliefs and students' motivation to learn.* Paper presented at the Annual Meeting of the American Educational Research Association, Chicago, IL.

Rueda, R., & Garcia, E. (1994). *Teachers' beliefs about reading assessment with Latino language minority students* (Research Report 9). Washington, D.C.: National Center for Research on Cultural Diversity and Second Language Learning. (ERIC Document Reproduction Service No. ED 376 721

Rumelhart, D. (1975). *Toward an interactive model of reading.* Technical Report No. 56. San Diego, Center for Human Information Processing, March 1976.

Rupley, W. H., & Logan, J. W. (1986). Relationship between teachers' beliefs about reading and their reported use of questioning and engagement strategies. In J. A. Niles & R. V. Lalik (Eds.), *Solving problems in literacy: Learners, teachers and researchers,* Thirty-fifth Yearbook of the National Reading Conference (pp. 165-170). Rochester, NY: The National Reading Conference.

Russell, T., & Johnston, P. (1988, April). *Teachers learning from experiences of teaching: Analyses based on metaphor and reflection.* Paper presented at the Annual Meeting of the American Educational Research Association, New Orleans, LA.

Russell, T., Munby, H., Spafford, C., & Johnston, P. (1986). Learning the professional knowledge of teaching: Metaphors, puzzles, and the theory-practice relationship. In P. Grimmett, & G. G. Erickson (Eds.), *Reflection in teacher education* (pp. 67-90). New York: Teachers College Press.

Sacks, C. H., & Mergendoller, J. R. (1997). The relationship between teachers' theoretical orientation toward reading and student outcomes in kindergarten children with different initial reading abilities. *American Educational Research Journal, 34,* 721-739.

Salinger, J. D. (1951). *The catcher in the rye.* Toronto, Canada: Bantam.

Schubert, W. H., & Ayers, W. C. (Eds.) (1992). *Teacher lore: Learning from our own experience.* New York: Longman.

Schulz, R. (1997). *Interpreting teacher practice: Two continuing stories.* New York: Teachers College Press.

Shanahan, T. (Ed.) (1994). *Teachers thinking, teachers knowing: Reflections on literacy and language education.* Urbana, IL: National Council of Teachers of English.

Shaw, C. R. (1930). *The jack-roller: A delinquent boy's own story.* Chicago: The University of Chicago Press.

Shogan, R. & Craig, T. (1964). *The Detroit race riot: A study in violence.* Philadelphia: Chilton Books.

Shulman, L. S. (1986). Those who understand: Knowledge growth in teaching. *Educational Researcher, 15* (2), 4-14.

Shulman, L. S. (1987). Knowledge and teaching: Foundations of the new reform. *Harvard Educational Review, 57,* 1-22.

Smith, D. M. (1983). Reading and writing in the real world: Explorations into the culture of literacy. In R. Parker & R. Davis (Eds.), *Developing literacy: Young children's use of language* (pp. 173-189). Newark, DE: International Reading Association.

Smith, R. W. (1994). Reflection—a means of critically evaluating prior school experience. *Educational Foundations, 8* (3), 17-32.

Soler, J., Craft, A., & Burgess, H. (2001). *Teacher development: Exploring our own practice.* London, UK: Paul Chapman.

Spong, J. S. (1991). *Rescuing the Bible from fundamentalism: A bishop rethinks the meaning of scripture.* New York: HarperCollins.

Spyri, J. (1945). *Heidi* (H. B. Dole, Trans.). New York: Grosset & Dunlap.

Steffy, B. E. (1993). *The Kentucky Education Reform: Lessons for America.* Lancaster, PA: Technomic.

Steiner, R. (1926). *The Christ impulse and the development of ego-consciousness.* London, UK: Anthroposophical Publishing Company.

Steiner, R. (1933). *The gospel of St. John: A cycle of lectures given at Hamburg, Germany, from 18th to 31st of May, 1908* (M. B. Monges, Trans.). New York: Anthroposophical Press.

Steiner, R. (1959). *Cosmic memory: Prehistory of earth and man.* Englewood, NJ: Rudolf Steiner Publications.

Stevens, G. (Director). (1959). *The diary of Ann Frank* [film]. (20th Century Fox).

Stodolsky, S. S., & Grossman, P. L. (1995). Subject-matter differences in secondary schools: Connections to higher education. *New Directions for Teaching and Learning, 64,* 71-78.

Stratton Lemieux, M. M. (1996). Teachers of young children: The moral dimension within our personal practical knowledge. *Dissertation Abstracts International, 56,* 4274A.

Stuart, J. (1949). *The thread that runs so true.* New York: Charles Scribner's Sons.

Stubbs, M. (1980). *Language and literacy: The sociolinguistics of reading and writing.* London, UK: Routledge & Kegan Paul.

Szwed, J. F. (1981). The ethnography of literacy. In M. F. Whiteman (Ed.), *The nature, development, and teaching of written communication* (pp. 303-320). Hillsdale, NJ: Earlbaum.

Tann, S. (1993). Eliciting student teachers' personal theories. In J. Calderhead & P. Gates (Eds.), *Conceptualizing reflection in teacher development* (pp. 53-69). London, UK: Falmer Press.

Taylor, C. S. (1990). *Dangerous society.* East Lansing, MI: Michigan State University Press.

Taylor, C. S. (1993). *Girls, gangs, women, and drugs.* East Lansing, MI: Michigan State University Press.

Taylor, D. (1983). *Family literacy: Young children learning to read and write.* Exeter, NH: Heinemann.

Taylor, D., & Dorsey-Gaines, C. (1988). *Growing up literate.* Portsmouth, NH: Heinemann.

Thomas, W. I., & Znaniecki, F. (1927). *The Polish peasant in Europe and America.* New York: Knopf.

Thorndike, E. L. (1917). Reading as reasoning: A study of mistakes in paragraph reading. *The Journal of Educational Psychology, 8,* 323-32.

Tolstoy, L. (1912). *Childhood, boyhood, and youth.* (C. J. Hogarth, Trans.). New York: Dutton.

Tompkins, J. P. (Ed.) (1980). *Reader-response criticism: From formalism to post-structuralism.* Baltimore: The Johns Hopkins University Press.

Trapedo-Dworsky, M., & Cole, A. L. (1996, April). *Teaching as autobiography: Connecting the personal and the professional in the academy.* Paper presented at the Annual Meeting of the American Educational Research Association, New York, NY.

Treloar, J. (1966a, September 25). The inner city classroom—A reporter's education. *Detroit Free Press,* pp. 1A, 10A.

Treloar, J. (1966b, September 26). Model student or problem? It could be up to teacher. *Detroit Free Press,* pp. 1A, 2A.

Treloar, J. (1966c, September 27). 'They're just dumb,' slum teachers say. *Detroit Free Press,* pp. 3A, 8A.

Treloar, J. (1966d, September 28). 2 different worlds brush in classroom. *Detroit Free Press,* pp. 1A, 4A.

Wagner, D. A. (1986). When reading isn't literacy (and vice versa). In M. E. Wrolstad & D. F. Fisher (Eds.), *Toward a new understanding of literacy* (pp. 319-331). New York: Praeger.

Wahlberg, D. (1996, October 30). Fraud case at U-M may spark expulsion. *The Ann Arbor News,* pp. A1, A8.

Wells, G. (1986). *The meaning makers: Children learning language and using language to learn.* Portsmouth, NH: Heinemann.

Weidler, S. D. (1989, February). *Exploring preservice teachers' knowledge structures about reading.* Paper presented at the Annual Meeting of the Eastern Educational Research Association, Savannah, GA.

Widick, B. J. (1989). *Detroit: City of race and class violence* (Rev. ed.). Detroit, MI: Wayne State University Press.

Willinsky, J. (2002). *After literacy: Essays.* New York: Peter Lang.

Wilson, S. M., Shulman, L. S., & Richert, E. (1987). '150 different ways' of knowing: Representations of knowledge in teaching. In J. Calderhead (Ed.), *Exploring teachers' thinking* (pp. 104-124). London, UK: Cassell.

Winikates, D. L. (1996). Becoming teachers of "learning disabled" children: Reflections on professional career paths and the development of critical awareness (Doctoral dissertation, University of Houston, TX, 1995). *Dissertation Abstracts International, 56,* 4733A.

Winner, I. P. (1978). Cultural semiotics and anthropology. In R. W. Bailey, L. Matejka, & P. Steiner (Eds.), *The sign: Semiotics around the world* (pp. 335-363). Ann Arbor, MI: Michigan Slavic Publications.

Wixson, K. K., & Lipson, M. Y. (1991). Perspectives on reading disability research. In R. Barr, M. L. Kamil, P. B. Mosenthal, & P. D. Pearson (Eds.), *Handbook of reading research* (pp. 539-570). New York: Longman.

Zeichner, K. M., & Tabachnick, R. B. (1981). Are the effects of university teacher education "washed out" by school experience? *Journal of Teacher Education, 32* (3), 7-11.

AUTHOR INDEX

SUBJECT INDEX

ABOUT THE AUTHOR

James Muchmore has taught reading, English, language arts, social studies, and special education in public schools in Kentucky and Ohio. A graduate of Vanderbilt University (B.S., M.Ed.) and the University of Michigan (Ph.D.), he is currently an Assistant Professor of Education at Western Michigan University, where he teaches courses in literacy education and qualitative research. His research interests include self-study, teacher development, student writing, and home schooling. He and his wife enjoy reading, traveling, watching movies, and spending time with their young daughter.